Modern Japanese House

Modern Japanese House

Modern Japanese House Naomi Pollock

In recent years commercial buildings have begun to look the same all around the world. Japan's are no exception. Made of glass, steel, and concrete, office towers, shopping complexes, and hotels in Tokyo bear a striking resemblance to their counterparts in Houston, Shanghai, and London. Houses, however, remain particular to place. Unique microcosms molded by local customs and social mores, the houses of one country are still distinct from those of another. They are stubbornly rooted in their own indigenous context.

The *shoji* paper screen is commonly used to define or separate space.

A steeply slanting tiled roof of a traditional Japanese house.

An interior view of the traditional post and beam structure.

In Japan, the very idea of "house" is not the same as in other countries. Many Japanese houses, and especially those designed by avant-garde architects, do not look, feel, or function like American or European homes. Some are oddly shaped or capped by steeply slanting roofs. Other houses feature rooms in unexpected places: A third-floor kitchen is practically inconceivable in the West, yet in Japan it happens all the time. No matter where they are located, all houses must provide shelter for sleeping and eating. Beyond those basic requirements, Japanese houses part ways with those from other points on the globe.

What makes the Japanese house distinctly Japanese are deeply ingrained usage patterns, social relationships, and a host of other contextual factors. Today's houses reflect both historical traditions and contemporary realities. More than worldwide trends, local conditions guide design decisions. In Japan, where land is limited and sites are small, building codes determine house shapes, and furniture dimensions fix room sizes. Architects put rooms where they fit, even if the location is not the most practical. Boundaries between home and business are often blurry, and residences housing dentist's offices, dry cleaners, and other commercial ventures are common. Construction materials are also unconventional. In this relatively forgiving climate, any raw material, even plastic or paper, is a potential building block.

The narrowest definition of "context" refers specifically to surrounding site conditions. In many European and American cities, codes and design guidelines strive for consistency among cornice line heights, uniformity of street walls, and compatibility of materials from one building to the next. In Japan, where buildings are treated as separate entities, these considerations are rare, and the only relevant definition of context is a broad one that incorporates many different conceptual, as well as physical, attributes. Limited and expensive land, treasured traditional culture, and changing social structure all have a strong bearing on the external appearance as well as the internal organization of the Japanese contemporary house.

The state of the built environment, especially in major Japanese cities, exerts surprisingly little influence on house design. Ever-changing backdrops and odd adjacencies are as much a part of the neighborhood scene as the local shrine or temple. Though Tokyo's urban infrastructure remains remarkably unchanged — for the most part its residential areas comprise blocks of tiny buildings bound by narrow streets — individual buildings are caught up in a never-ending cycle of demolition and reconstruction. They come down and go up practically overnight without a thought to shared architectural vocabulary or stylistic continuity along the street. On many residential streets, the only constant is the steady march of electricity poles.

These circumstances naturally spawn a certain amount of visual chaos and leave architects with little foothold for design. Yet they also free architects to build much as they please. If the house next door is likely to be torn down, there is no reason to engage it in any aesthetic or formal dialogue with the adjacent structures. Its replacement could be a convenience store, video-rental store, or some other equally unsightly neighbor. For many architects, the best defense against this threat is simply to build a wall around their house.

Having survived natural disasters, war, and massive urban renewal, the country is used to rebuilding. Individual buildings, and especially houses, have a life expectancy of only about twenty years — a big difference from the United States, where hundred-year-old houses are fairly common, or Europe, where they are even older. After two decades, many Japanese houses show considerable wear and tear and are ripe for *tatekae*, or scrapping and building. In Japan, where few buy used goods, the market for secondhand homes is limited. Though these structures are valued for their beauty and cultural significance, very few people want to live in them, since they tend to be dark, drafty, and difficult to maintain.

Legal constraints, rather than physical context, tend to fix building size and position. Says architect Koh Kitayama, "The width of the street in front determines the building's height—the narrower the street, the lower the house." Though variances are possible, small sites are often made even smaller by height limits and setback restrictions. In addition to the usual lot line and street front setback rules, the so-called sunshine laws curtail the number of hours a building may cast shadows on its neighbors. Occasionally, additional setbacks are required for anticipated street widening at a usually unspecified time in the future.

Zoning and building restrictions help keep development and density under control. In Japan, and especially in Tokyo, where the cost of real estate remains very high, land is money, and existing buildings have very little value. "This creates an incentive to turn residential properties into moneymakers," laments architect Nobuaki Furuya. Not only developers but landowners of all types subdivide their property. In the United States, families may choose to sell the house when a property-owning parent dies, but in Japan, many families must sell part of their holdings just to pay the exorbitant inheritance taxes.

This explains in part why sprawling estates with gardens and private teahouses are rare, especially in Tokyo. Prior to World War II, homes, or *ie,* large enough to accommodate an extended, multigeneration family were common countrywide. Traditional Japanese houses had a number of common characteristics. Most were carefully composed horizontal arrangements of corridors and rooms between a high thatch or tile roof overhead and a level floor plane below. Room sizes and proportions were determined by modular systems spawned by the structural column grid and the dimensions of the *tatami* straw mat. Though mat sizes varied according to region and time period, all were related to the proportions of the human body: One *tatami* mat was roughly the size of one person.

Between the ceiling and floor, an assortment of fixed and movable walls, translucent paper *shoji* and opaque *fusuma* screens, partitioned the space but also could be pushed aside to enlarge rooms. This element lent itself to remarkable functional flexibility, especially when paired with movable furniture. By stowing the *futon* mattresses and sliding a table and cushions into their place, one could instantly transform sleeping quarters into a sitting room. Adding a screen or a flower arrangement elevated it to a reception room for guests.

By contrast, some rooms had very proscribed purposes. Places considered unclean, such as the kitchen and toilet, did not serve multiple functions. While cooking usually went on in the *doma,* a dirt-covered area below the level of the living space's raised floor, toilet use took place in a room of its own, completely separated from the bathing area, which was considered clean.

Of course, all this changed drastically after World War II, when shifts in the family structure were reflected in house planning. "In the prewar period, a big family needed a big house," explains architect Hiroshi Maruyama. "But in the postwar period, the family broke down into smaller units." Though typically the eldest son took over the family business and homestead as before, his younger brothers, who were left to fend for themselves, increasingly headed to the city to seek their fortunes. To meet the needs of these new arrivals and their nuclear families, the Japanese government began to build subsidized apartments, and the "nLDK" planning system was born. The term, borrowing from English, refers to "number of bedrooms, living room, dining room, kitchen." Instead of specifying room size only, the new nomenclature also assigned roles to different spaces. A typical 3-LDK layout meant an apartment or house with three *tatami* rooms, a kitchen, and a living/dining room area.

Inspired by the Western idea of one room for one function, the new system was intended to upgrade the quality of living conditions by separating communal and sleeping areas and dividing the home into several small rooms. "It became the gauge for all types of living units," explains architect Yoko Kinoshita. "But then it took over, and no one stopped to evaluate the system."

It was also thought to generate the perfect home for postwar Japan's idealized social unit: the nuclear family composed of a couple plus children. In contrast to the prewar extended family led by a dominant patriarch, the postwar family was far more democratic and seen as an "incubator for children," according to architect Jun Aoki. "After the war, children were valued more, not just by their parents, but also by the nation as a whole."

Though initiated by the government, the nLDK system caught on with private homebuilders and developers, including the so-called housemakers or specialized house manufacturers that began introducing their products in the 1960s. Borrowing the idea of assembly-line manufacturing, these companies used standard patterns and stock parts to design and build houses. Modeled after suburban American homes, these new homes did not require designs by independent architects.

Today housemakers have a large stake in Japan's private-home market, especially in large metropolitan areas like Tokyo and Osaka. Many even have warranties and maintenance services that last long after construction is complete. Selected from company catalogs, Web sites, and showrooms, the houses come in a wide range of plan types and styles — picket fences, pass-through kitchens, and *tatami* mat guestrooms are all among the options. "What people are buying is the image presented by the housemaker," says Tokyo architect Chiharu Sugi. "But that image differs from the reality." The English Garden model may have built-in planters and trellises, but any likeness to its namesake stops there.

Another drawback of prefabricated houses is that they do not adapt easily to the irregular site and social conditions that are increasingly common in Japan. That said, the housemakers' shortcomings can result in opportunities for architects. Clients with small or awkward properties often consult architects with the design skills to turn pitfalls into innovative dwellings.

The owners of Small House, an 829-square-foot (77-square-meter) house in the heart of Tokyo, might have been able to fit a housemaker unit on their 646-square-foot (60-square-meter) lot. Ultimately, the couple wanted something more distinct, so they hired architect Kazuyo Sejima to build their unique home. The jewel-like, metal-clad building was completed in 2000. The interior is divided among four stacked levels, each different in size and ceiling height. The

Japanese housemaker houses are modeled on typical suburban American homes.

Traditional sliding *shoji* screens divide interior rooms.

Kazuyo Sejima's Small House in Tokyo.

The facade of Yasuhiro Yamashita's Lucky Drops in Tokyo.

Sir Norman Foster's Century Tower is a landmark in Tokyo's contemporary urban landscape.

Tadao Ando's 4 x 4 House (right) faces a panoramic view of the Inland Sea and Awaji Island.

tilted walls resulted from connecting the levels and accommodating the tiny plot hemmed in on two sides by neighboring houses.

Changing social demographics are another reason why clients are consulting architects. Currently, only 60 percent of Japanese households fit the mold of the conventional nuclear family, according to Kinoshita. As in developed nations everywhere, single parents, unmarried couples and other nontraditional definitions of family are on the rise. In addition, while Japan's elderly population is increasing, its birthrate is lower than ever. In June 2003, the *Nihon Keizai Shimbun* reported that for the first time the number of births countrywide dropped below 1.3 children per family and in Tokyo to an all-time low of less than one child per family.

The implications of these changing conditions for house design are significant. Architects are increasingly asked to create homes that meet or anticipate the physical needs of older clients who would like to live independently or with their grown children in multigeneration homes. Single people with no intention of ever marrying and childless couples without plans to become parents are also hiring architects. With the resources to spend on home design, many of these householders want, and can afford, homes tailored to their needs and lifestyles.

The unmarried and the childless are just one segment of Japanese society with disposable income. Despite periods of economic fluctuation, the country as a whole has become steadily more affluent since 1945. Though designer homes constitute less than 1 percent of the market, according to Kyoto architect Waro Kishi, designers have benefited from this growth.

The hiring of an architect is not a privilege of the wealthy alone. In Japan it can be an option for people of lesser means as well. Interest rates have been very in low in Japan for years, making mortgages affordable. The most restricted projects are often the most innovative, requiring architects to rethink conventional structural systems, construction materials, and spatial organization.

When a thirty-year-old couple found an inexpensive narrow strip of land for sale by the Tokyo city Waterworks Department, they sought approval from architects Yasuhiro Yamashita and Masahiro Ikeda. "What the client wanted to know was not what they could build on this land but whether they could build on it at all," says Yamashita. Ninety-four feet long (thirty meters long) and covered with fiberglass-reinforced plastic, the house, which was completed in 2005, "looks like a chopstick," says Yamashita. Its name, Lucky Drops, is a translation of the Japanese version of the expression "saving the best for last."

Japan's wealth has also contributed to improved design quality. A country with a rich history of producing exquisite objects, Japan has an inherent appreciation of beautifully crafted goods. But it was the economic bubble period of the late 1980s that stimulated a wider interest in contemporary architecture. During that time, Japan underwent a major building boom led by landowners who put up office complexes, condominiums, and luxury hotels with astonishing speed. In the process, architects foreign and local were put to work. Poorly designed and shoddily built, many of these projects were blatant moneymaking ventures. Others, such as Sir Norman Foster's Century Tower, completed in 1991, made significant contributions. Collectively they raised the quality of building design countrywide and called attention to contemporary architecture in ways that had never occurred before in Japan.

The Japanese media have become strong promoters of architecture and design to the general public. Television shows devoted to architect-designed houses air weekly, and neighborhood bookstores are richly stocked with monthly magazines and books dedicated to the subject.

Casa Brutus, a trendy magazine devoted to good design, conducted a survey in 2000 among its 120,000 readers. The readers were asked to select their favorite architect from a list of ten candidates and send the editors a short description of their ideal home. The magazine then directed the responses to the respective architects to see if a match could be made.

Eighty people gave Osaka architect Tadao Ando top ranking. Ultimately, a site owned by a concrete contractor from Kobe caught Ando's eye. This small segment of land was bordered on the north by railroad tracks and a two-lane highway and to the south by a spectacular view of the Inland Sea and Awaji Island — the epicenter of the Great Hanshin Earthquake that jolted Japan in 1995. Taking advantage of the seascape but turning its back on the traffic, Ando's 4 x 4 House was completed in 2003. It is a four-story tower made of the architect's signature material, concrete.

As 4 x 4 attests, artistic freedom tempered by tough conditions stimulates the architect's creativity. "Architecture is not fine art," says Shigeru Ban. Too much freedom, either economic or artistic, does not necessarily bring out the best in architects. In post-bubble-period Japan, where the two seem to be in balance, architects have built some of the most inventive houses in the world

Organized by five typological categories, Japanese architect designed homes of the past fifteen years are the subject of this investigation. This volume explores an array of structures built to accommodate the contemporary client in diverse domestic and environmental circumstances. These house types are not unique to Japan; yet each one is distinctly Japanese.

At 1,076 square feet (100 square meters), the average home in Tokyo is quite small. Yet many couples and even families of three or four happily make do with less, especially in Tokyo, where conditions are so extreme that small apartments or tiny houses are often the only choices. By contrast, the average single family home in the United States contains about 2200 square feet (204 square meters) and houses two to three people.

The exterior of Takamitsu Azuma's Tower House in the heart of Tokyo.

A traditional Japanese *chanoma* featuring *tatami* mats, *shoji* screens, and an *irori* hearth.

In Japan, where there is no such thing as a minimum-size lot, glorified one-room living areas or a series of vertically stacked rooms, each one hardly bigger than a postage stamp, are what many people call home.

For Japanese, a small living space does not necessarily connote deprivation. On the contrary, Western homes seem too big to many residents of Japan. "Whether a house feels small or not depends on a person's experience," says architect Hitoshi Abe. In Japan, where there is a rich history of tiny contemplative tearooms, floor area has nothing to do with quality of space. While insufficient storage and excessive clutter are perennial problems for denizens of tiny houses, their spiritual comfort level is completely dimensionless. A sense of belonging and the price of ownership are the priority. Awareness of other family members — a difficult feat in a big house with fixed walls and firmly shut doors — is for many one of the most desired features, taking precedence over personal space and privacy.

While living in a tiny house requires certain concessions, the Japanese lifestyle is very forgiving and easily adapted to homes of any size. At a minimum, houses contain places to cook and gather, sleep, bathe, and use the toilet. Larger homes have more rooms or embellished versions of this basic set. Whether big or small, all homes in Japan are private retreats where strangers seldom venture. Though the social divide between inside and out is clear and formal, borders within the home, where spaces interlock and functions overlap, are fuzzy and fluid. Even in mass-produced apartments, there is a preference for rooms that flow into one another, often separated only by movable partitions.

The heart of most houses is the all-purpose *chanoma*, or its contemporary equivalent, the combined kitchen-dining-living room. Here family members gather to eat, watch television, do homework, and engage in social activities. Though the traditional *chanoma* was *tatami* covered, today it is more likely to have a wood or carpeted floor. Whether furnished with *zabuton* cushions or Western-style chairs, the room is frequently equipped with movable pieces that can be rearranged as needed. Foldable furniture coupled with functional flexibility makes for very efficient use of any space no matter its size.

By contrast, the purpose of designated sleeping areas — bedrooms, sleeping lofts, or *tatami*-floored cubicles — is primarily rest. In Japan it is common for entire families to share beds or *futon* until children reach elementary-school age — a space-saving device and social custom all in one.

Bathrooms are often divided into independent bathing and toilet areas that can be used by different people at the same time. This lessens or eliminates the need for a second bathroom and even permits the separation of tub and toilet if there isn't enough room for them side by side.

To compensate for their small homes, many people today disperse their living space among several different geographic bases throughout the city. "It's not possible to do everything in one house," explains architect Manabu Chiba. Schools, offices, and parents' homes often provide additional storage, study, and socializing spaces to augment the small dwelling.

Many residents also expand their usable area by taking advantage of the city's resources. Coffee shops, bars, and restaurants double as living rooms where guests are entertained. *Sento* public baths, and now health clubs, practically eliminate the need for a shower at home. Convenience stores are fast becoming the city dweller's kitchen. And playgrounds and public parks serve as everyone's backyard.

While today most people who want to reside in Tokyo have no choice but to live in apartments or small houses, others couldn't imagine it any other way. "I like the city life," says architect Takamitsu Azuma. "I like to meet people, and have access to new information, traditional culture, and the many things that happen in the city spontaneously." Though Azuma could have built his own home on a large suburban lot, he chose a 220-square-foot (20-square-meter) triangular site fronting Kira Dori, a four-lane artery built in preparation for the 1964 Olympics held in Tokyo. Running through the heart of Tokyo, Kira Dori slashed the grid of the existing residential neighborhood and left many triangular plots in its wake. When completed in 1967, Azuma's five-story, 700-square-foot (65-square-meter) Tower House was the only residential property on the street and "probably the smallest house in the world designed by an architect," says Azuma.

Though one of a kind, Tower House became a symbol of a new brand of *toshi jutaku*, or urban dwelling, characterized by small size, verticality, and defensive street walls. The emergence of *toshi jutaku* coincided roughly with the rapid developments that accompanied the Olympics and the 1970 Expo in Osaka. These houses were in part a reaction to the urban infrastructure upgrades that came at the expense of residential enclaves, as well as an alternative to suburban developments, whose houses were meant to lure people away from the city with generous floor plans and gardens.

While Tokyo's mid-century growth spurt changed the fabric of the city, these modifications were modest compared with the massive rebuilding after the Great Kanto Earthquake in 1923 and World War II firebombs that leveled most of the city. These disasters could have yielded opportunities for urban planners, but instead reconstruction in many neighborhoods followed the lines of the tiny plots and narrow streets laid out during the Edo period (1600–1868). Though the buildings were new, the network of streets and walkways binding them together echoed the past.

Tokyo's cramped conditions may be rooted in its history, but the pace of crowding picked up considerably following World War II, when people flocked from the country to the city in search of employment. As Tokyo's population rose, new forms of housing, such as speculative or government-subsidized apartment buildings, emerged. Large luxury apartments in Tokyo are a recent phenomenon and, priced in the millions of dollars, are an option only for the very rich. The steady migration to Tokyo and other large cities contributed to the incessant cycle of more and more people trying to live on less and less land.

Because land values have dropped from the bubble-period highs of the late 1980s and early 1990s, home building has become a viable option for some who could not afford it before. Though construction in Japan is expensive, those costs are small compared with the still, extravagant cost of land. Consequently, assuming available land can be found, many can buy only a tiny or oddly shaped parcel of land in a peculiar location.

Increased demand, coupled with high property values, has created a market for smaller and smaller parcels. "Fifteen years ago, 100 square meters (1,076 square feet) was considered small," says Manabu Chiba. "But over the past five years, houses have become even smaller. Now 70-square-meter (753-square-foot) houses are being built." Contributing to this trend, developers carve up their holdings into as many pieces as possible.

Aside from the city of Tokyo's required 6.5-foot (2-meter) minimum street frontage for emergency vehicles, access, there are very few legal restrictions governing the shape of lots. That said, a host of code regulations designed to protect the public from natural disasters, such as fires and earthquakes, as well as to control the impact of new construction on the surrounding area, often significantly inform building shapes. In addition to laws limiting site density, the sunshine laws are the most critical code issues for designers of small houses in Tokyo. Based on the belief that everyone is entitled to a certain amount of sunlight each day, the laws limit the number of hours a building may cast a shadow on neighboring properties and thoroughfares. Calculated according to the angle of the sun at winter solstice, the laws not only dictate building setbacks, height, and volume but also account for the multitude of steeply angled roofs crowning both commercial and residential properties throughout the city.

In response to tight conditions and strict requirements, many architects start by determining the permissible building envelope and then work their way inward. Once that external parameter is established, there are many different ways to divide the interior space. While client and architect accept the house's small size, most designers still look for ways to maximize what they have.

"I ask myself where I can double up spaces," says architect Sugiura Denso. Assigning multiple uses to one room is a logical solution, given Japan's tradition of multipurpose, flexible space. By keeping functional roles loose, architects help their clients prepare for inevitable changes in the family constellation, such as the arrival of a baby or the departure of a child once he or she reaches adulthood.

There is rarely enough room for everything the clients request; thus prioritization is a must. Usually the nonessentials, such as Western-style living rooms and *tatami*-floored guest rooms, are the first to be eliminated. "We must determine the most important space for each family," says architect Jun Aoki, "and then base our design around that."

Once the project's programming stage is complete, most architects use various strategies to make the small house feel larger. For some, not being able to see around a corner makes a room feel bigger. Others argue that space should be divided as little as possible — the sum total of lots of little rooms does not equal one big one.

Within the legal and site restrictions, architects try to extend their buildings in whichever direction possible. Though some architects find ingenious ways to attach balconies and other flourishes exempt from the code's area calculations, most expand vertically. Due to significant land shortage, the city of Tokyo decided to exclude underground space from the total tally in the late 1990s. "By using the below-grade space, we can nearly double the size of the house," explains architect Tomoaki Tanaka. Though it is a blessing to some architects and homeowners, others shy away from building below grade because it is expensive and can be difficult to realize as high-quality usable space. There are also very few precedents for it in Japan. "I don't like to use underground space," says Takaharu Tezuka. "The ground should stay as it is for our descendants." Instead, many architects expand upward. While the code may limit rooftop enclosures, roofs often become exterior outlets for drying clothes or recreation.

Within the small house, vertical expansion helps offset cramped quarters. "If you have a small site, you need height," says architect Satoshi Kurosaki. Where there is no choice but to stack rooms vertically instead of horizontally, the staircase assumes the role of corridor or hallway, often access-

The narrow configuration of a typical Edo period street plan.

ing a single room at each level. By varying ceiling heights, it is possible to establish spatial hierarchy. Maintaining low ceiling heights and optimizing floor levels is architect Yoshinari Shioda's strategy for maximizing usable square footage, though other architects gladly trade floor area for double-height ceilings and void spaces that add a sense of expansiveness to almost any size room.

At the other end of the spectrum, miniaturization or dimension reduction may add precious inches. Architects of tiny houses often brush up against the minimum staircase and corridor widths required by code. Puzzling out ways to make walls as thin as possible, use the smallest structural elements, or even install the tiniest bathroom fixtures available may result in marginally bigger rooms. While adopting these extreme measures is sometimes a matter of choice, often it is necessary.

If all else fails, the power of suggestion can make rooms in even the smallest house appear larger. A skylight framing a personal view of the sky or carefully placed windows to catch cross-breezes can link a confined space to the boundlessness of the natural environment outside. Architect Denso Sugiura believes that every little house needs a big tree. "The tree can be appreciated from bottom to top: the trunk from the first floor, the branches from the second, and the leafy shade from the third," he explains. Highlighting even the subtlest natural phenomena draws attention outside of the four walls, and even the most tenuous connection to the ever-changing world outside animates an interior.

External exposure must be weighed against protecting privacy. Houses are often built very close together in Japan, thus visual and audial privacy can be difficult to achieve. Unique level changes that prevent windows from aligning with those next door, opaque materials that let light in but maintain privacy, and buffer zones such as entry foyers are familiar techniques for separating the client from the neighbors.

To gain further privacy, clients sometimes request inwardly oriented homes. While courtyards are not common in small houses, they are not entirely unheard of either. One of the most influential postwar houses, Tadao Ando's Sumiyoshi Row House, completed in 1976, pushed the courtyard concept to an extreme. "My intention was to insert a concrete box and to create within a microcosm," explains Ando. The house occupies an oblong site in central Osaka, hemmed in by wood row houses on either side. Completely shutting out its surroundings, the house fronts the street with a blank concrete wall punctuated only by a single door. It conceals a tripartite plan with a small courtyard at the center that separates two blocks of living space. Though it opens the interior up to the sun and sky, the exterior space requires its owners to go outside to get from bedroom to bath and living room to dining room. "For us, the facade, the courtyard, and the

concrete itself were shocking," says architect Waro Kishi.

Within the small house, privacy and personal space are often hard to come by. "Privacy in Japan means you can't be seen from outside," says Aoki. Indeed, more often than not, privacy within the Japanese home is a state of mind more than a state of being. "There are two ways to achieve privacy," explains Abe, "through physical isolation or mental isolation." By choosing not to see and not to hear, it is possible to draw a boundary, if only an imagined one.

While architects and clients have their ways of coping with the lack of privacy and personal space, practical constraints, such as a lack of storage space, often baffle even the most talented designers. Although many architects are experts at carving out storage — inside the staircases, under the *tatami* mats, or within built-in cabinetry and shelves — it is often insufficient. This shortage poses a serious problem in a country as materially rich as Japan. "The trade-off is always a big room with no closets versus a small room with lots of closets," laments architect Hiroshi Maruyama. Architects such as Akira Yoneda may urge their clients to dispose of unnecessary possessions before moving in, but less trafficked rooms in the Japanese home often evolve into places to store belongings, since attic and basement storage areas are uncommon.

Despite these and other challenges, many Japanese cling to the romantic vision of a house of their own, no matter how small. This desire calls on architects to reorder the customary elements of the home and redefine what it takes to turn a shelter into a home. Complex conditions, such as an extreme shortage of space, often spawn some of the most creative solutions.

The center courtyard of Tadao Ando's Sumiyoshi Row House in Osaka provides a light-filled outdoor passageway between rooms.

Opposite: The house's unadorned facade masks the maze of rooms inside. The modest front door, capped by a canopy of thin steel plate, leads the way inside.

Right: Compensating for the son's bedroom's narrow width — just big enough for a bed — and making the most of the soaring ceiling height, Sejima punctured the outer wall with a large picture window high enough to preserve privacy but low enough to frame an interesting street scene.

Far right: Covered with grass mats, the third-floor sitting room is an isolated retreat. Wall openings connect it to the double-height master bedroom and library one floor below.

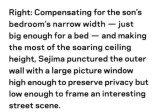

Though the name House in a Plum Grove conjures idyllic images of delicate blossoms and leafy branches, this boxy little building, completed in 2004, stands on a corner lot in suburban Tokyo, bounded by two narrow streets, a pocket-sized playground, and a parking garage. That said, the connection to trees is not by name only. The last piece of a large subdivided agricultural property, this plot was dotted with plum trees when purchased by the clients — a couple in their thirties. While they hoped to hang on to the flowering foliage, they also wanted to maximize the use of their tiny 990-square-foot (92-square-meter) plot. Though drawn to the idea of one-room living, the family also needed a home where they could coexist amiably with their two children, mother, and pet cat. Architect Kazuyo Sejima's resolution of these goals is a benign-looking three-story house encircled by eight plum trees — nearly enough to call a grove.

From the outside, the house exudes an ephemeral quality typical of Sejima's architecture. Behind its blank facade is an interior full of surprises. The most astonishing feature is that it contains twenty-two distinct rooms, including storage and staircase hall. Instead of combining functional elements, Sejima coped with limited space by dividing it as much as possible. Though the rooms are essentially rectilinear, their proportions are out of the ordinary: Some are tall and narrow, others long and skinny, and all are very small. Despite the complexity of both plan and section, the rooms fit compactly together inside the tidy white box.

The ground floor holds an entry hall, a Japanese-style room for the client's mother, a kitchen, a double-height dining room, and the son's bedroom. The son's bedroom has a ceiling that ascends 14 feet (4.2 meters) overhead and a floor area not much bigger than the bed itself. A double-height shelf-lined library, the master bedroom, the daughter's bedroom, and studies for both children — each barely big enough for a desk — fill the second floor. Above that, a sliver of a bathroom runs along one side of the house and a tatami-floored tearoom opens onto an enclosed, grass-covered roof terrace. The terrace leads to yet another sitting room, this one a private retreat for one or two people. Though this little room is physically separated from the others by an external entrance, an inner window visually connects it to the library one floor below.

Stuffing so many rooms into a building of this size could not be achieved using conventional walls. Instead, Sejima substituted 0.6-inch (16-millimeter) steel sheets that are a mere fraction of the thickness of standard wood frame plus wallboard partitions. Even though the exterior walls were padded with a layer of insulation and coated with reflective paint, they are only 2 inches (50 centimeters) thick, still considerably thinner than their Western counterparts. This strategy not only saved valuable inches, it eliminated the need for an independent structural system altogether, since the steel sheets are more than strong enough to hold up the house. Another advantage to the steel

Right: Ground-floor plan.

Overleaf: Instead of asking her clients to divest their extensive library, Sejima made a place for their books on the second floor. Full-height shelves and an Eames chair contribute to the cozy atmosphere.

walls was the ease of their construction. Built from the inside out, the house was first anchored by a steel post that forms the core of the spiral staircase. After that it only took a few weeks to bolt together the factory-made interior and the exterior walls on site. Once properly positioned, the walls were permanently welded together.

While the steel partitions clearly separate each room, windows, wall openings, and entryways (there are no internal doors) connect them. Throughout the house, air, sound, and light flow freely, joining rooms to rooms and floors to floors. Though the daughter's second-floor bedroom is the same size as her bed, internal windows open the cozy berth to the study on one side and, on the other, to the dining room one floor below. From there a *nijiriguchi* doorway, modeled after the entrance to a traditional tearoom, connects to the grandmother's quarters. The small, square opening only inches from the floor is an awkward passageway, but it enables grandmother and granddaughter to communicate without having to shout.

Drilling holes in the steel panels to hang pictures or other artwork is not an option, but the clients quickly figured out that magnets could be used to hold up calendars, shopping lists, and posters. Sejima carefully placed openings in the walls so almost every room has something interesting to look at. Carefully positioned to preserve privacy, each window looks out at the street, up toward the sky, or into an adjacent room such as the library, with its iconographic faux-wood-grain wallpaper. The thin, white walls distort the sense of depth rendering each room a photographic snapshot: crisp, focused, and flat. Instead of masking everyday objects, the white walls enhance the clients' many possessions. In this house, furniture, food packages, surfboards, and other objects of daily life add color, detail, and scale.

"Carefully positioned to preserve privacy, each window looks out at the street, up toward the sky, or into an adjacent room such as the library with its iconographic faux wood-grain wallpaper."

House in a Plum Grove; Kazuyo Sejima & Associates; Tokyo

Left: Stark white walls and a concrete floor provide a neutral backdrop for the clients' Western-style antique dining set. A large window opens onto the garden, illuminating the space.

Below: The boxy little house is all but oblivious to the garage next door and the ubiquitous above ground telephone wires in front.

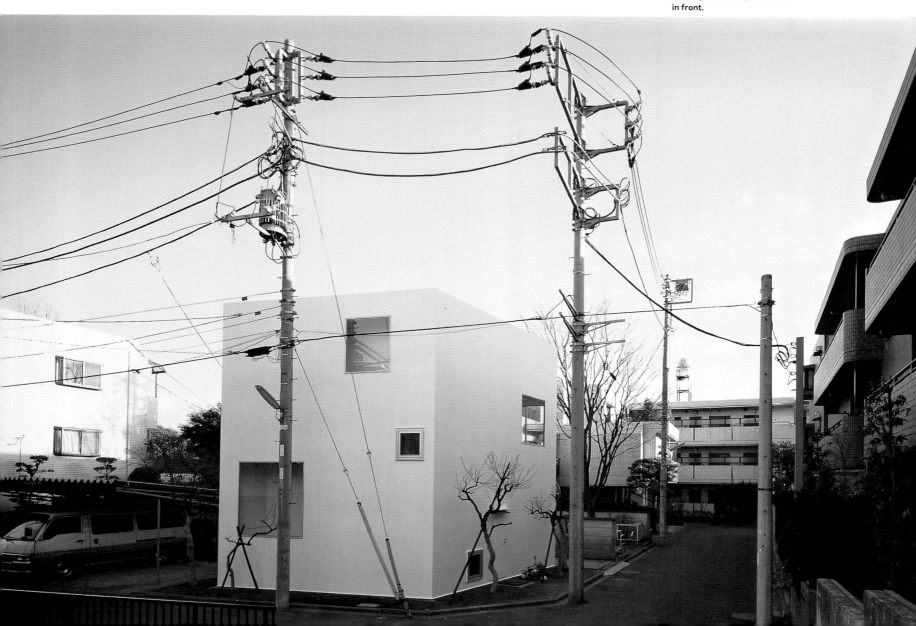

Above: Generous wall openings connect the daughter's bedroom to her study on one side and the dining room one floor below on the other.

Right: Sections.

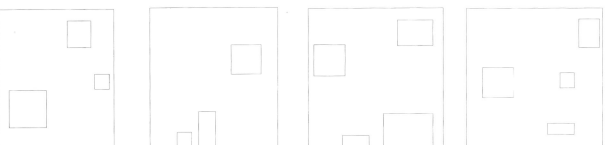

12·13

Opposite: Though cool and anonymous by day, the facade glows warmly at night when the interior is illuminated. Here, the front door, which is suspended from above, is open.

Some houses are small. Others are practically invisible. An 800-square-foot (74-square-meter) dwelling on a flag-shaped site in suburban Tokyo, c House is almost completely boxed in on all four sides by neighboring buildings. "It is almost like a secret space," says the house's architect, Jun Aoki. "You can't even see the site from the road."

Completed in 2000, "c" is one of six houses that now fill a site where one house once stood. A 6.5-foot-wide (2-meter-wide) gravel-covered strip just big enough to accommodate a car tethers the facade to the street. The face of the building is windowless, set back from the street, and sandwiched between housemaker houses on either side. Only 54 inches wide (137 centimeters wide), the entire facade is not much bigger than the front door. Made of metal paneling to blend with the building base, the door is barely identifiable as the entrance to a house. Though anonymous by day, at night its translucent fiberglass panels glow like a giant lantern.

Inside, a small patch of floor is used for exchanging shoes for slippers. Here the ceiling soars to 14 feet (4 meters), adding a touch of grandeur to an otherwise tight space. Steep steps make a clean break with the outside world and lead up to the main floor. At the top of the stairs is the open kitchen, the pivot point of the L-shaped plan's wings. One wing contains the living room, and the other holds the pantry, followed by the wife's atelier. With its Western-style sofa, piano, television set, and coffee table, the wood-floored living room looks the part but acts more like a traditional *chanoma*. While eliminating a dining area was easy since the clients, a young couple with a small child, prefer to eat seated on their couch, it was also a useful space-saving measure. Separating living room and kitchen, a second set of stairs leads down to the lower level, where the master bedroom and toilet occupy one wing and a second bedroom, followed by a walk-in closet, washroom, and Japanese-style bath, fills the other.

Though most designers of tiny houses try to use as few partitions as possible, Aoki did the opposite at "c" by squeezing in eleven rooms. "A one-room space will feel smaller than one divided into many distinct areas," explains the architect. Strung together like links in a chain, Aoki's rooms lead directly to rooms, but doors in between separate one from the next. A level change divides the first-floor private quarters from public ones above, and both floors contain a mixture of "main" and "back" rooms or support spaces. Distinguished by function, finishes, and square footage, each room is like a new discovery.

"In every house, we start by determining the most important space for the family and then design around it," says Aoki. For "c" the garden clearly took precedence. In contrast to the warren of rooms inside, the 18-by-9-foot (5-by-6-meter) square of greenery is practically expansive. The clients wanted a private outdoor retreat where they could entertain guests and they urged Aoki to provide as large an exterior space as possible. "If the clients didn't want an outdoor space, they would live in an apartment," explains the architect. At the expense of making a tiny living space even tinier, Aoki framed the garden by the house's two wings, where it is open to an unobstructed view of the sky. It benefits from the site's secluded position and is visible from every room in the house.

Naturally, windows and garden views relieved the sense of confinement inherent in a tiny space. Floor-to-ceiling transparent panes held in place by thin lines of steel sash, the windows are just one element in the palette of planar surfaces, textured materials such as knotty pine and ceramic tile, and rectilinear built-ins that Aoki used to articulate the house's boxy rooms. While beige tones and warm wood floors identify the "main" rooms, gray paint and white acrylic panel characterize the pantry, closet, and other "back" spaces. Shimmering galvanized-steel panels in the staircase enclosure add yet a third vocabulary. Abstract and devoid of scale, Aoki's materials do not draw attention to the house's small size. Together with the house's minimal details and concealed structural elements, the materials underscore the dwelling's clear lines and smooth surfaces.

Although the structural wood columns are embedded in the exterior walls, a thin wood veneer disguises the floor slab. A mere 6 inches (15 centimeters) deep, the structural steel deck had the added benefit of reducing the floor thickness and the overall building height to 18 feet (5 meters) — a good 3.28 feet (1 meter) shorter than its neighbors. Unlike most tiny-house designers who try to expand vertically, even if only with a void space, Aoki lopped off centimeters wherever he could keep ceiling heights to a minimum, floors thin, and the building close to the ground. By lowering the house, Aoki maximized the garden's daylight and sunshine.

Sacrificing ground both horizontally and vertically for the sake of the garden might seem counterintuitive when habitable space is at such a premium. By default, most Japanese houses sit in the middle of the site and use the leftover space as the garden. Design strategies for the flag-shaped site are even more limited. In congested settings like this one, it is easy to overlook empty space. By using the house to define the size and shape of the garden and vice-versa, Aoki strikes a pleasing balance between built form and open greenery.

Opposite: Set back from the street and crowded by housemaker houses on either side, the front door is easy to miss.

Top right: Overlooking the garden, the living room is where the family congregates. Steel-clad stairs lead down to the lower-level sleeping quarters. A freestanding island separates the kitchen area and keeps pots and pans from view.

Right: Hinged steel panels act like casement windows, letting in fresh air.

Far right: Main floor plan (top); lower-level plan (center); longitudinal section (bottom).

Overleaf: The two wings of the L-shaped house shelter the garden. A variety of fixed and operable, transparent and opaque panels bind interior and exterior together.

Pages 32–33: Galvanized-steel stairs connect the public living area above with the family's private domain below (left). A narrow, steel-clad corridor leads from the stairs to the light-filled master bedroom overlooking the garden (right).

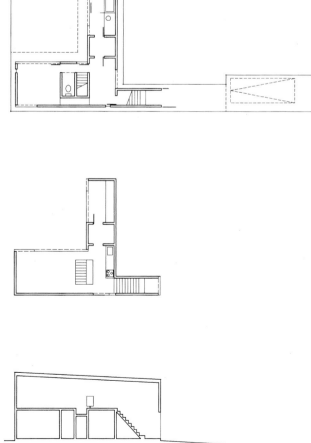

"At the expense of making a tiny living space tinier, Aoki framed the garden by the house's two wings, where it is open to an unobstructed view of the sky."

c House; Jun Aoki & Associates; Tokyo

"Shimmering, galvanized-steel panels in the staircase enclosure add yet a third vocabulary."

c House; Jun Aoki & Associates; Tokyo

When architects Masaki Endoh and Masahiro Ikeda collaborated on the design of Natural Shelter, an 829-square-foot (77-square-meter) house in the heart of Tokyo, they were deeply concerned about protecting the property's cherry tree from damage during their new construction. The architects recognized that incorporating views of the land's lush foliage and spring flowers allowed them to fill the tiny house with a wonderful atmosphere — a benefit well worth the exchange for square footage.

Natural Shelter successfully replaced the owner's traditional-style wood house built shortly after the end of World War II, with a contemporary structure that honors the property's lush landscape. Shaped like an enormous, curving bow embedded in the earth, the new house is perched above a massive retaining wall that separates it from the busy street 20 feet (6 meters) below. Completed in 1999, it consists of three levels: entry, kitchen, toilet, and living room on the first floor; bath, washroom, sunroom, and storage on the second; and a recreation room on the third. At the south end of the house, a glass-enclosed void runs the entire height of the building, allowing air and sound to move freely between levels. Within this slot of space a metal-grille spiral staircase connects balconies at all floors, each one oriented toward the cherry tree.

Preserving the neighbor's tree was not the only challenging site condition facing the designers. The most significant limitations were the existing houses hemming in the 581-square-foot (54 square-meter) property on three sides. In fact, the air space above the road is the only open area near the house. Cramped quarters were a small price to pay considering this residential enclave's remarkably central location. Despite its convenience, the neighborhood eludes developers because many local residents choose to rebuild instead of move out.

The clients wanted a new house where they could live comfortably with, but independent from, their adult son; they also wanted to retain the spatial quality of their old home, a two-story building with one multipurpose room on each floor. This functional flexibility of the old house was a means of coping with the property's small size. But the clients happily gave up their old house's *tatami* flooring — getting up and down from the mats can be very hard on elderly bodies.

Accustomed to making due without much personal space, the clients felt at home with their new residence — a space loosely divided into one level per family member. Though the son largely occupies the top floor, the father the second floor, and the mother the first, their areas overlap in the shared kitchen and bathrooms. Within each level, furniture divides the space and enclosed, private rooms were avoided — even the second-floor tub and toilet are enclosed by glass.

By dividing each level as little as possible and using glass instead of opaque walls if separation was needed, Endoh and Ikeda maximized floor area and allowed daylight

Opposite: Glass from top to bottom, the south elevation of the house opens the three-story interior to light and view.

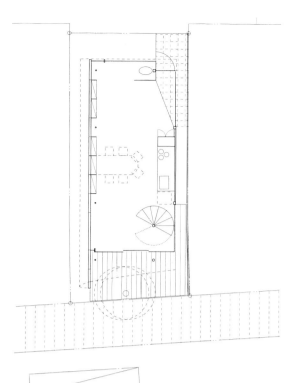

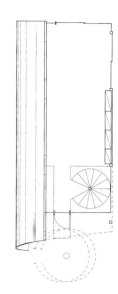

Right: First-floor plan (left); second-floor plan (center); third-floor plan (right).

Below left: Facing the street, the house's outdoor spaces become progressively smaller toward the top floor.

Below right: At the rear of the house, the ground plane drops off precipitously.

Opposite: The first-floor front door
opens directly into the combined
living/dining room and kitchen.

to penetrate the full length of the house. "Because of the small plot, it was impossible to make lots of rooms," explains Endoh. Wrapping the bathroom with glass provided little privacy but allowed the room to be smaller without feeling too confined. As a result, even bathers can enjoy the cherry tree. White surfaces and blond-wood flooring complement the open interior and contribute to the overall light and airy atmosphere.

The proximity of neighboring houses restricted the placement of exterior glass but inspired the architects' innovative structural solution. An important space-saving device, the design eliminated the need for a secondary substructure for support. The curved side of the house contains plates measuring no more than 3 millimeters (0.1 inches) thick, carrying structural load and keep out cold. On the flat side, slender steel beams and columns double as the framework for cement wallboard panels. Supplementary beams and braces, all painted white and reduced to their minimum dimensions, complete the system. Another benefit of this method was that the two narrow, non-load-bearing end elevations could be composed as the designers saw fit. While the house's west end is all glass, its eastern entry side is mostly covered to protect the clients' privacy.

Although the house's curved shape is a striking statement — visible even from taxis racing past on the street below — it was a direct response to specific site conditions. Not only does it satisfy the code requirements, limiting how much shadow the top of the house can cast on its neighbors, it also establishes a respectful distance between its foundations and those of the adjacent home. While that separation was necessary on the ground level, on the second floor the curved profile widens the room but cinches back in toward the top of the house. Within the room the arched wall restricts movement slightly, but the constant awareness of the overall volume makes the house seem bigger. In the tiny house the power of suggestion can be as important as, or even more important than, utilizing every square inch. Curved walls and void spaces may come at a cost, but on balance they add more than they take away.

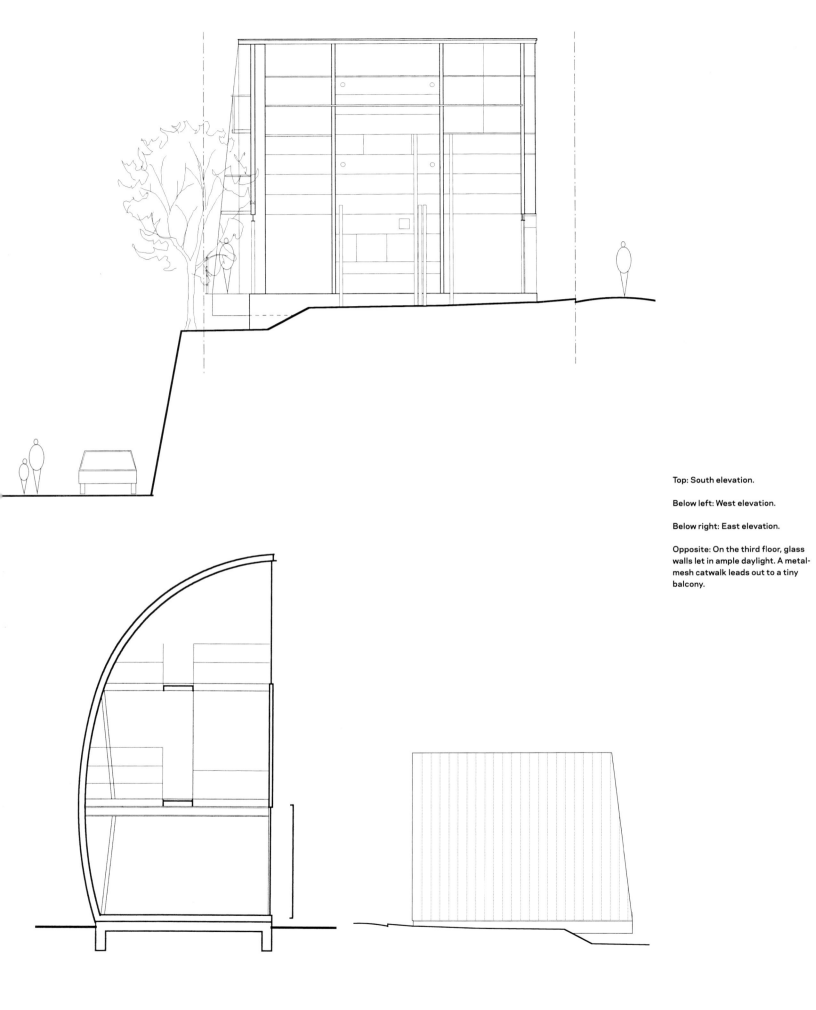

Top: South elevation.

Below left: West elevation.

Below right: East elevation.

Opposite: On the third floor, glass walls let in ample daylight. A metal-mesh catwalk leads out to a tiny balcony.

"By dividing each level as little as possible and using glass instead of opaque walls if separation was needed, Endoh and Ikeda maintained floor area and allowed daylight to penetrate the full length of the house."

By any standards, UNS, a single-family home in central Tokyo, occupies a highly desirable site. It's close to a major shopping hub yet abuts a quiet residential neighborhood. With parks and easy access to the city's vast transportation network nearby, this property appears ideal. Yet, like so many residential plots in central Tokyo, this one is not just small: At a mere 614 square feet (57 square meters), it is tiny.

Despite this severe restriction, architect Hiroyuki Arima managed to accommodate a lot of features into this very tight lot. A parking spot, albeit only big enough for a Rover Mini, and a rental office or studio occupy the ground floor; a *nando* (all-purpose room used for storage) and guest quarters with its own entrance compose the second floor; the third floor features a combined dining room/kitchen and living room/ gallery; above that, a bathroom and roof terrace; and, perched at the very top, a meditation room for one.

While the site's size may not have fazed the client, a furniture-company executive who travels constantly, it posed numerous challenges for the architect, a native of Fukuoka. A city on the southern island of Kyushu, Fukuoka has plenty of land, and its residential neighborhoods are considerably less congested. Arima was glad to try his hand at designing for one of Japan's increasingly common, yet ever-perplexing, tiny urban sites.

Arima's first space-saving idea was to pare down the structural system to small, closely spaced columns along the building's front and back faces. This arrangement kept side elevations and the internal space entirely column free and enabled Arima to use partitions very selectively. It also meant he could make them out of any other non-load-bearing material. To distinguish one room from another, Arima relied on level changes — seven in all — that preserve continuous vertical as well as horizontal space.

Hugging the rear wall, a wide, skylit staircase takes up almost a third of the plan. This is square footage well spent. The staircases' white surfaces, floating treads, and minimal enclosure make ceiling heights, which run as low as 7 feet (2.1 meters) in the dining area, less noticeable and visually extends adjacent rooms. On top of that, a skylight overhead opens onto a dramatic view of limitless blue sky, filling the stairwell, as well as every room it touches, with daylight.

For Arima, a pacific garden respite was the priority. This was difficult to accomplish because of the narrow but busy shopping street in front, neighboring houses only inches away at the rear, and the ever-present threat of new construction next door. In addition, the aboveground train tracks are well within hearing and sight.

Unable to forge a connection with the outdoors at the bottom of the building, Arima did so at the top. Far removed from the street-level commotion, the sun-drenched bathroom, with its potted plants, wood floor, and glass roof, is a semioutdoor oasis in the middle of the city. The exterior is wrapped on two sides by a terrace that acts as a protective buffer and is also an ideal spot for sunbathing. A densely

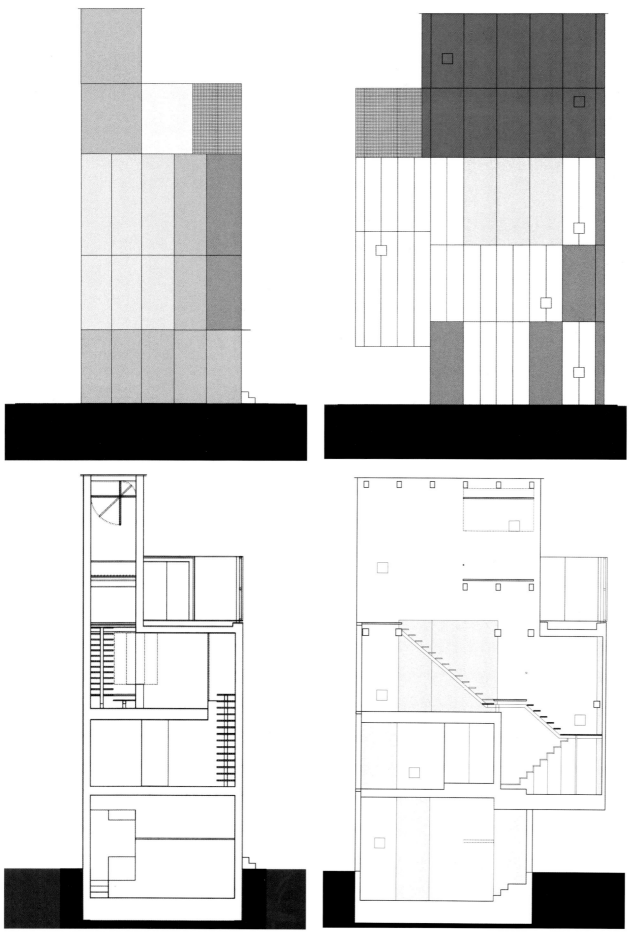

Top left: Elevations showing exterior panels.

Bottom left: Sections.

Opposite: A world unto itself, the rooftop bathroom is a sun-drenched oasis opening onto a private, wraparound terrace.

"Far removed from the street-level commotion, the sun-drenched bathroom, with its wood floor, and glass roof, is a semioutdoor oasis in the middle of the city."

UNS; Hiroyuki Arima; Tokyo

woven metal screen — material normally used to enclose baseball diamonds — shields the terrace. The metal mesh provides a comfortable degree of enclosure and thwarts prying eyes.

Although a huge skylight would let in plenty of natural light, the client still had to be able to look outside. In anticipation of inevitable redevelopment nearby, Arima devised a double-layered building skin that can be reconfigured for privacy, if any fast-food shops or apartment towers go up in the vicinity. Inspired by traditional translucent *shoji* paper screens and exterior wooden *amado* panels, Arima's version consists of wood, stainless steel, polycarbonate, and glass rectangles of various levels of transparency, that can be mixed, matched, and rearranged to edit views and protect the interior as needed. Some panels let in diffuse light, others frame oblique views toward the street or include operable windows to ensure adequate cross-ventilation.

"The staircases' white surfaces, floating treads, and minimal enclosure make ceiling heights, which run as low as 7 feet (2.1 meters) in the dining area, less noticeable, and visually extends adjacent rooms."

UNS; Hiroyuki Arima; Tokyo

"Though the first house largely obscures the second, the architect had to consider the needs of both houses and establish harmonious social and visual relationships between them."

T Set; Chiba Manabu Architects; Tokyo

Previous pages: T Set is the second of two adjacent houses designed by Chiba. The first house occupies the front of the site, where it juts out toward the street. T Set stretches across the back of the property (left). The front door is tethered to the street by a narrow walkway (right).

Opposite: Enclosed in a black wood box, the kitchen is treated like an oversize piece of furniture.

Right: Stairs ascend from the mezzanine level to the top floor bedroom.

Though there is no minimum house size in Japan, there is a minimum size for livable space. At 646 square feet (60 square meters), architect Manabu Chiba's flag-shaped house in a residential Tokyo neighborhood is close to that limit. Everyone has an individual tolerance level for constricted space — in Japan 323-square-foot (30-square-meter) efficiency apartments are common — but furniture has to fit. If mattresses and tables are too short or too low, the users' basic needs cannot be met. Even *futon* bedding, which can be folded up and stowed away, must comply with standard size criteria.

Measuring a mere 10 by 30 feet (3 by 9 meters), this house was completed in 2002. The structure, the second of two adjacent homes, sits tucked behind the first home, completed for a young couple six months prior. Given the extreme site conditions and paucity of space, the architect had no choice but to use furniture dimensions and placement to determine room sizes in the phase-two house. This basic approach helped ensure that the entire house, as well as each of its component pieces, would be small enough to fit on the tiny site but big enough for comfort. These relatively objective standards were also useful since the house started out as a developer's speculative project, devoid of the usual client likes and dislikes that normally guide design decisions.

Essentially, the house is a rectangular white block containing two small black wood-covered boxes. Straddling the line between furniture and architecture, one black box holds the first-floor kitchen and bath. Its top doubles as a mezza-

nine-level sitting area that leads up to the second box containing the two top-floor bedrooms. Multifunctional and circulation spaces, such as stairs, corridors, and the 136-square-foot (12.6-square-meter) double-height combined living and dining room, fit around the two boxes. Attached to the main body of the house is a narrow corridor, just wide enough to align with the 35-inch-wide (90-centimeter-wide) front door. Loaded along one side with built-in storage, this conduit doubles as the *genkan* entry foyer.

Code requirements demand clear access to the house entrance from the street in case of emergency. This strip of land, only 9 feet (2.8 meters) across, wide enough for a walkway and a parking space, directly links house and street. Slightly taller than its neighbors, the house is hemmed in on the better part of its four sides. Operable windows and large expanses of glass at either end fortify its connection to the outdoors by filling the house's cramped quarters with daylight, breezes, and views out toward the road.

To preserve privacy, Chiba discreetly positioned all windows and entryways. Though the first house largely obscures the second, the architect had to consider the needs of both houses and establish harmonious social and visual relationships between them. Like a carefully choreographed dance, glass does not open onto glass, and gray exterior walls — galvanized steel for phase one and painted stucco for phase two — blend together yet retain their individual identities.

"Operable windows and large expanses of glass at either end fortify its connection to the outdoors by filling the house's cramped quarters with daylight, breezes, and views out toward the road."

Opposite: The narrow entry foyer leads to the double-height living room, whose tall ceiling and large windows glow in the evening.

Living in such close proximity is not uncommon among family members, but the owners of these two houses were not even friends. They became business partners when they purchased the property together. This unusual relationship came about when the young couple wanted to acquire the entire property but could not afford to buy it outright. While smaller parcels could be had elsewhere, most were poorly proportioned or awkwardly shaped. The couple compromised by splitting this land with their real-estate agent, who developed his share, phase two, with the intent to sell it one day.

The initial proposal divided the site down the middle, with two long, narrow houses side by side. This did not agree with Chiba, who is ever mindful of the pattern of solids and voids that define Tokyo's unique urban character. "That kind of division is too closed and does not encourage interaction with the city," he explains. Instead, the architect proposed building the houses perpendicular to each other, one in front of the other. While the rear house, phase two, stretches across the site, the front house is centered on the front property line, flanked by open space. Although a mere 31 inches (80 centimeters) separates Chiba's two houses, the side lots act as a buffer between the front house and its neighbors on either side. Despite his careful planning, even Chiba was shocked by the second site's small size. "It looked like the backyard," he says.

Right (clockwise from top left to right): First-floor plan; elevation; mezzanine-floor plan; second-floor plan; section.

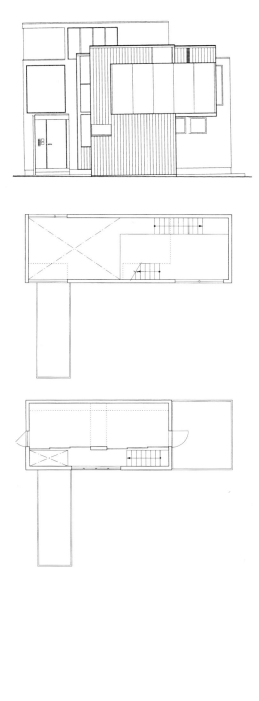

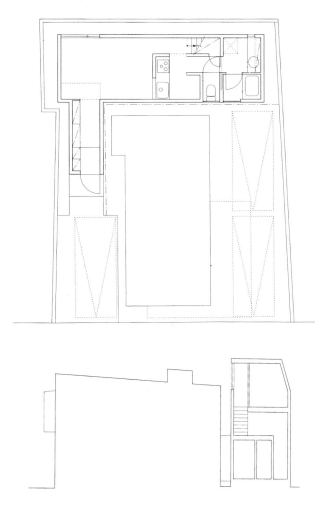

Houses are meant to shelter people from the elements. The appropriate balance between contact and protection is an individual matter, but these proclivities are often tied to culture and climate. The integration of the outdoors in contemporary Japanese houses is rooted in spiritual beliefs and practical solutions derived from traditional house types such as *minka*, or rural houses, and *machiya*, or urban merchants' houses.

Japan's shift from an agricultural to industrial society after World War II undoubtedly weakened the historical connection between housing and the natural environment; yet even shrinking sites, increased density in the nation's cities, and the consequent lack of privacy have not completely severed the tie.

The amiable relationship between house and environment stems from a number of sources, including the fundamental belief in the integrity of man and nature, a basic tenet of Zen philosophy. The spiritual connection, coupled with premodern Japan's available construction technology, spawned a close bond between the home and its natural context. This bond is manifest in the country's two basic forms of residential architecture: the house enclosed by garden and the garden enclosed by house.

Detail of a roof beam made from a curved tree trunk in an Edo period home.

Historically most houses in Japan fell into one of these categories or, especially in the case of large homes, blended both. Space and social stature permitting, homes were surrounded by land. "We lived in the garden as well as the house," explains architect Jun Aoki. Unlike the West, where houses and gardens were often built in sequence, in Japan they usually developed in tandem and were composed as one: The garden helped define the house and vice-versa. Whether adjacent to the house or contained within it, the garden was considered an integral part of the house.

Fastidiously maintained and trimmed, the formal Japanese garden carefully comprises greenery, stone, and water elements ringed by walls, fences, and other demarcations. Restrained, edited, and sanitized versions of nature meant mostly to delight the eye, Japanese gardens are entirely different from the exuberant English variety riddled with footpaths and brimming with flowers of every hue. Japan's refined, private oases belonged largely to the rich. Others of more moderate means had to make do with more modest renditions. Even simple homes were often fronted by small gardens intended to distance the house from street activity.

A traditional *engawa* porch.

Over time, the ways people live and build in Japan have changed dramatically, especially during the postwar period, when new and improved methods and materials made it easier to control the quality of interior space. Though house builders today have a multitude of choices, during the Edo period (1600–1868) carpenters used readily available materials and construction technology. Regardless of the owner's social stature or the location of the house, most dwellings were made from fragile local materials. Though the palette varied

according to regional availability and style, the materials were assembled into a fairly standard set of building blocks that included clay walls, wood floors, and a variety of movable wood or paper screens. The quality of craftsmanship and level of refinement depended on the owner's wealth and social standing, but the basic kit of parts was the same. The frame comprised a matrix of wood beams and columns, while walls, floors, and roofs provided enclosure. Traditional post-and-beam construction was very flexible, separating structure from shelter, and allowing carpenters to put openings almost anywhere they wanted.

Since traditional houses relied heavily on passive heating, cooling, and lighting, the freedom to strategically place windows and movable walls was critical. Equally important was the positioning of the house. To properly ventilate a house required windows on two sides. To make the most of the sun's warmth, large windows and movable walls had to be concentrated on the house's south side.

Whether they lined an exterior perimeter or interior garden, large openings that could be opened or closed at will were essential for light and air but also resulted in ambiguous borders.

"In the traditional house, there was no rigid separation between in and out," says Aoki. In addition to sliding outer walls, all houses were equipped with habitable, transitional spaces that bridged the gap between interior and exterior, such as *genkan* entry foyers, *doma* dirt-floored work areas, and *engawa* verandas. Regardless of placement, abrupt transitions between inside and out were avoided.

A uniquely Japanese feature, the traditional *engawa* was a narrow, wood-floored porch common to both country and—space permitting—city houses. It was sheltered by deep roof eaves overhead and sandwiched between sliding screens made of translucent *shoji* paper on the inside and protective wooden *amado* on the outside. A functional space in its own right, the *engawa* was a place to share a casual cup of tea with a neighbor or attend to simple chores while basking in the sunshine. By day both sets of panels could be pushed back, turning the *engawa* into an extension of the interior room that flowed effortlessly into the garden. When the house was closed for the night, the two sets of screens could be shut, turning their shared pocket of air into insulation and the focus of the room inward.

Within the house, the *doma* vestibule acted as an internal buffer between interior and exterior. Contiguous with the ground plane but below the floor level of the house, the earth-floored *doma* was where outside shoes were removed before one stepped up to enter the house. A multipurpose space, the *doma* was used for a variety of activities considered less clean, such as storage, cooking, and, in the case of farmhouses, agricultural tasks. Though the *doma* is no longer a common feature, today's *genkan* entry foyer retains the level change and shoe exchange but is used as a place to greet outsiders without compromising the privacy of the home.

In many city homes, *doma*-like vestibules were important bridges between inside and out. In *machiya* town houses, long, narrow buildings usually hemmed in on either side by neighbors, the *doma* was the first in a string of rooms interspersed with tiny gardens, or *tsuboniwa*. They not only separated the family quarters from street activity but also provided a forum for merchant homeowners to conduct their commercial transactions. With little or no space between houses, perimeter gardens and porches were not possible. Instead, the courtyard gardens preserved the spiritual connection to the outdoors and satisfied the practical need for fresh air and daylight.

Set within the overall framework of the house, the *tsuboniwa* is a tiny enclosed patch of greenery measuring about a *tsubo*, or 35 square feet (3 square meters). Miniature orchestrations of plants and small trees accented by stone ornaments, *tsuboniwa* were not intended for circulation like the habitable courtyards found in other countries. Joined to living spaces by movable screens, the *tsuboniwa* was meant to draw hot air out of the house. "Making a window is an easy way to let air in but generating wind in static architecture . . . that is the function of the *tsuboniwa*," says architect Satoshi Okada. In densely populated areas where there was not room for both house and expansive greenery, or in large homes where perimeter sources of light and air could not penetrate interior rooms, enclosed gardens were both practical and aesthetically pleasing.

It is often said that the openness of Japan's architecture came about in response to the country's forgiving climate. Japan may be more temperate than the United States and northern Europe, but its climate, which spans Hokkaido's nearly Siberian winters at one extreme and Okinawa's tropical weather at the other, is hardly uniformly hospitable. Aptly named, Japan's Snow Country in the middle of the country gets an astounding 10 feet (3 meters) of snow each year. In the Kanto plain and Kansai district, where most of the population is concentrated, there are four distinct seasons. While the arrival of winter fruits or summer blossoms are causes for celebration, the accompanying changes in temperature are not always so welcome.

At its extremes, Japan's weather is not always easy to bear, but people in Japan tend to be more tolerant of intense heat and bone-chilling cold. While the openness of traditional houses was well suited to summer highs, they could be drafty and downright uncomfortable in winter. During this weather, an *irori* hearth, *hibachi* portable heaters, and layers of thick clothing were the primary defenses against plummeting temperatures. All of these devices were intended to heat the person, not the room.

Even today, when mechanically controlled heating and cooling systems are readily available, few choose central systems over unit heaters or air conditioners. "We don't like to heat or cool the entire house, [only where there are people]," explains architect Shigeru Ban. Set on timers, individual appliances can be activated without anyone ever needing to wriggle out of their *futon*. A *hanten* padded jacket, thick socks, and a cozy perch under the *kotatsu*, the essential quilt-covered electric foot warmer, can cure any remaining chills.

To combat heat in warmer weather, traditional houses not only opened on at least one side via movable walls but also were elevated nearly one foot (30 centimeters) above ground so fresh air could circulate beneath the floor. Residents who still prefer natural ventilation and a direct connection with outside conditions happily endure warmer temperatures without resorting to mechanical systems that chill the air. Even when summer's heat and humidity are at their worst, there is always a modicum of airflow. Though insufficient to cool the body, it is enough to elicit a gentle tinkle from the ever-popular *furin* chimes hung from roof eaves or window frames. To many Japanese, the mere sound connotes a cooling breeze. While a paper fan and an iced drink help, coping with Japan's heat is a mental as well as a physical process.

Although traditional attitudes toward integrating the outdoors may be at the heart of many contemporary homes, the surrounding environment has now changed almost completely. Since the close of World War II, technological advances and social changes, such as the dissolution of the extended family and mass migrations from country to city, have influenced the division and development of land. The profound impact of increased Westernization on the way people lived, or thought they ought to live, was also significant.

These and countless other forces eroded the historically ideal relationship between indoor and outdoor space, or altered it practically beyond recognition. Still, many people cling to traditional paradigms, at least in concept. "Today everybody wants to live like the rich, with a house and garden of their own," says Aoki. "It's democratic but impossible." Stubbornly homeowners hang on to architectural bits and pieces, often pushed and pulled until they take on a new form, shape, or function that fits. The monolithic apartment blocks scattered all over the country may not have gardens, but every unit is equipped with a balcony, preferably on the south side, to air dry laundry and freshen *futon*.

A *doma* dirt-floored work area with *kamado* stove.

Japanese *tsubinowa* offer aesthetically pleasing climate control at the center of traditional homes.

A traditional *kamado* stove.

Underside of a traditional thatch roof.

Interior connects with exterior in Tezuka Architects' Machiya House in suburban Tokyo.

The living/dining room and *engawa* porch of Tezuka Architects' Wood Deck House in Kanagawa Prefecture.

Even for those who can afford to live like *samurai*, it is extremely difficult to build a large house and garden in Japan, especially in the middle of Tokyo. Not only are big parcels of land difficult to come by and prohibitively expensive, surrounding site conditions can be difficult at best to control. If a neighbor's kitchen window is only inches away, wall openings in a new house must be calculated and positioned carefully. Addressing known conditions is easy compared with anticipating how the neighborhood will change in the future.

Many city dwellers avoid these uncertainties by turning their back on them. Wrapping homes with high walls and focusing them inward are common coping mechanisms. Often architects find courtyards the ideal solution. Finished with wood floors and retractable roofs, today's courtyards are much more versatile than their historical precedents. Many have become habitable places and physical extensions of the home. Yui and Taka Tezuka's Machiya House in suburban Tokyo even has a giant bathtub, complete with hot and cold taps where their policeman client can loll about when off duty.

Courtyards are appealing in part because of their sunlight and sky views. Despite rampant development in Japanese cities, average building heights have remained low, a critical factor for keeping street-level shadows in check. Though courtyard houses may seem unfriendly, they may actually improve neighborly relations by putting distance between houses. In the past, a strong sense of community in residential areas dictated appropriate neighborly conduct providing a sense of security for some, yet it was suffocating for others. Though many housewives and retired gentlemen still sweep the street in front of their homes each morning out of courtesy to their neighbors, social change is weakening the sense of community and affecting domestic architecture.

Faced with unwanted external intrusions and odd adjacencies, architects in Japan use windows cautiously but wherever possible: high, low, or in the middle. Clerestories or glass panes that hover just above the floor direct attention either up to the sky and treetops or down to a patch of greenery and artfully placed bed of stones. Either device forges a visual link to the outdoors but blocks the eye-level view of the gas station next door. If all else fails, there are always skylights, a popular method to let in natural light, especially when no other source is possible. "We feel the exterior atmosphere in interior space through the use of ambient light," explains Tokyo architect Akira Yoneda.

To cope with noise and unsightly surroundings, many architects divide windows into two categories: one for view and another for ventilation. Though this is not a new technique, the reasoning behind it has changed. To let in air and create cross breezes, small bamboo grilles were often set into the mud walls of traditional houses. Today small, unobtrusive windows, frequently hinged at the top, allow in fresh air without compromising privacy.

Another reason for a greater degree of enclosure today is comfort. Simply put, fresh air and sunshine are restorative, but vermin and bugs are not. "One hundred years ago, we didn't care about bugs," says Aoki. "It wasn't so convenient, but we slept inside mosquito nets." Today, contemporary homeowners install window screens as a matter of course. No matter how light or diaphanous, screens draw a distinct line between inside and out.

Still, many people are unwilling to sever that all-important link to nature just because of a few insects. Designed by the Tezukas, the Wood Deck House hangs over a tree-filled valley that turns into a mosquito breeding ground as soon as the warm weather arrives. Above all, the owner wanted a house that maximized the land's magnificent view of a protected, government-owned ravine. The Tezukas oriented the back of the house toward the forested valley and created an open interior atmosphere by avoiding visual impediments, including screens. Except for one slender column, they not only eliminated all structural elements at the rear of the house but opened it up completely to a broad deck. Wrapping the house on two sides, the deck is a seamless extension of the combined living and dining room. Covered by a rolling canvas awning, it is like a traditional *engawa*, as much a part of the interior as an exterior space can be.

Very few homes in the Tokyo metropolitan area today enjoy comparable views. For most residents, a garden of any size is a true luxury. In general, wherever there is empty space on a property, people plant on it. Even the narrowest of residential walkways, barely wide enough for a person to pass, may be lined with potted plants and miniature *bonsai* trees, each one lovingly nurtured.

"Made of horizontal glass strips held together by sturdy aluminum frames, the shutters are both walls that can be locked securely into place and windows that can be opened."

Shutter House for a Photographer, completed in 2004, is the latest project from architect Shigeru Ban. Designed for a client who dreamed of "living with nature" in the heart of Tokyo, it is a checkerboard of courtyard gardens and contained interior rooms linked by floor-to-ceiling glass shutters. These transparent horizontal panels can be stacked up and stowed away above the ceiling, completely eliminating any vertical barriers between inside and out. Built from conventional glass and steel, this house is as radical as the Tokyo designer's earlier works made from honeycombed cardboard and paper tubes.

While Ban had been experimenting with shutters for some time — this is his fourth architectural application of a technology normally used for airplane hangars and garage doors — he had used them only for perimeter walls. This house was his first opportunity to try them in a courtyard setting within a building. At the outset of the project, the client, a commercial photographer with a keen interest in modern architecture, did not know about Ban's obsession with shutters. In fact, he was not familiar with Ban at all, before an exhaustive search for the perfect architect to blend garden with house and workplace with home led him to the innovative designer.

The first step toward realizing the project was finding a suitable site. Together, architect and client searched for a property in the residential neighborhood where the client, his wife, and their three children lived at the time. They settled on a long, skinny plot with a four-story condo-

minum across the street, an embassy complex behind and large homes all around. Despite the proximity of neighboring buildings and the narrow street frontage, Ban felt the land was rife with possibilities.

Taking his cue from the site's oblong shape, Ban proposed building a modern version of the traditional Kyoto-style *machiya* town house, usually composed of a string of rooms interspersed with a garden or two. Instead of this linear organization, Ban covered the site with a field of cross-shaped, steel columns laid out in a tartan grid and filled it in with a mixture of indoor and outdoor spaces. "If I used a simple square grid, it would be impossible to fit in all the functions," explains Ban. Composed of rectangles of different proportions, this system gave Ban tremendous flexibility and enabled him to make rooms big enough for the client's collection of modernist furniture and small enough to enclose a spiral staircase.

Within the grid, the rooms were positioned in relation to the house's four gardens: three internal courts and one tree-laden yard that doubles as a privacy buffer at the rear of the site. Like links in a chain, the primary rooms wrap around the largest of the courtyards. Designed by the client, the 258-square-foot (24-square-meter) garden boasts an artful arrangement of Japanese maple trees, green ground cover, and a traditional stone lantern. "If I had not become a photographer, I would have been a gardener," the client explains.

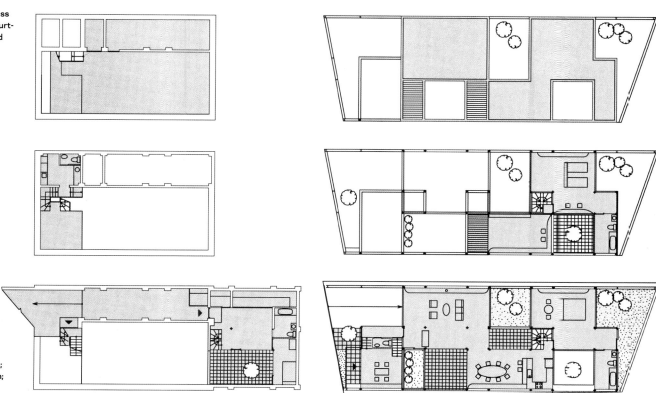

Right (clockwise from top left): Second basement plan; roof plan; second-floor plan; first-floor plan; mezzanine plan; basement-level studio.

The first courtyard is immediately visible on one's entrance into the foyer, acting as the transition point between public and private, and between office and home. Here steps lead down to the basement-level studio, a 20-foot-high (6-meter-high) white box with a darkroom and office to one side, or up to the double-height living room on the first floor. The living room connects to the dining room that opens onto the kitchen, a compact slot of space with a big window. The master suite is the final room at the back of the house. Facing three gardens, the shadowy bedroom is practically surrounded by greenery. The children's second-floor bedrooms above are as light and airy as a tree house.

Though the size and function of each room is specific and well defined, Ban's "Universal Floor" unites them into a single entity. Unlike Mies van der Rohe's Universal Space linked by a shared ceiling, Ban's concept is to connect with a continuous floor. "It's a traditional Japanese idea, only [my version is] a little more drastic," explains the designer. In traditional houses, sliding screens temporarily divided rooms, and the common floor plane ended at the eaves line. In Ban's house, the shared floor incorporates both indoor rooms and outdoor gardens.

While a sense of structural fluidity appealed to the client, he was unsure about the glass shutters. Would movable walls provide ample shelter? Would the glass panes withstand Japan's typhoons? Despite these initial concerns, the client ultimately agreed to five shutter walls. Made of horizontal glass strips held together by sturdy aluminum frames, the shutters are both walls that can be locked securely into place and windows that can be opened. "Buildings are like clothes," explains Ban. "They should change with the season." During the winter the focus of the floor-heated living room is its fireplace. Come spring, the shutters are opened, formality is shed, and the border between interior and exterior becomes ambiguous.

Within the house, walls are made of glass, allowing light and view to penetrate from one side to the other. Even the two bathrooms face courtyards with picture windows. Though privacy inside was not a primary concern, separation from the outside world was a requirement. To accommodate neighbors on both sides, the two long elevations are clad in opaque cement board interspersed with five "vertical gardens." Repeating the checkerboard pattern, each garden wall is composed of alternating squares of ivy. Nurtured by daily watering with an automatic irrigation system, the vines are expected to cover their metal supports completely and provide "translucency in a different way," says Ban.

By contrast, the two end walls are primarily glass, the rear screened by trees and the front by a woven metal screen covering the top of the facade. A later contribution, the white screen was designed concurrently with Ban's addition to the Centre Pompidou, Paris, whose undulating roof was inspired by a hat made of woven bamboo strips. While it

limits visibility and implies that the place beyond is private, the screen, in typical Japanese style, does not completely block views. Rather, it depends on the willingness of the passing pedestrians not to look too closely.

The idea of building a house with removable exterior walls is a product of Ban's unfettered creativity. It also required limitations set by the client. "Without constraints, I could not make architecture," says Ban. "The client had to let me find my own solution." He adds, "But if he had given me too much freedom, I could not have designed this house."

"Within the grid, the rooms were positioned in relation to the house's four gardens: three internal courts and one tree-laden yard that doubles as a privacy buffer at the rear of the site."

Shutter House for a Photographer; Shigeru Ban Architects; Tokyo

Opposite: Towering over its neighbors, Ambi-Flux hardly looks like a house at all. Concealed behind its blank white facade is the family's front door.

Below: Front elevation.

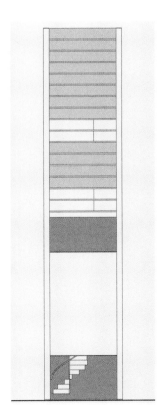

The design of Ambi-Flux included two seemingly straightforward client requests for a private garden and plenty of natural light. Though these were hardly unreasonable requirements under normal circumstances, the 13-foot-wide (4-meter-wide) site, squeezed between a *kushiage* restaurant and a bicycle repair shop and fronting a heavily trafficked thoroughfare, was anything but ordinary, even by Tokyo standards.

Situated at the heart of Shinbashi, a centrally located commercial neighborhood once famous for its Western-style tailors and furniture makers, the new house was completed in 2001. The structure had to fit into the existing Meiji-period (1868–1912) grid — a scheme comprising block on block of tiny shops and residences. In the original grid, merchants and their families lived in cramped quarters behind or above the store, and private gardens were not possible. Gradual redevelopment has contributed to the disappearance of these family-owned stores, and new construction has largely filled the existing footprints. Indeed, Ambi-Flux is no exception to this trend. Any other likeness to its surroundings stops there.

A stark, white, five-story "pencil" building, the house towers over its immediate neighbors. In keeping with the area's commercial character, it greets the street with two floors of rental offices. The residence itself begins on the third floor, with a single loftlike space running the house's entire 59-foot (18-meter) length. A small sitting area at one end, containing an easy chair, computer terminal, and child's dollhouse, segues into the dining area, where the family frequently congregates around their custom-designed table easily within sight and earshot of the open kitchen at the rear.

The house is equally fluid in section. At its center, a void stretches from tabletop to rooftop 39 feet (12 meters) above. A combined atrium and circulation core, the void divides the upper-level floors into two parts yet links every room with the elegant metal staircase wrapping its perimeter. The cantilevered steel steps lead up to the children's room and a storage vault on the fourth floor and then continues up to the family bath on one side and the master bedroom on the other side of the fifth floor. From there a spiral staircase ascends directly to the tiny rooftop garden — an oasis of greenery set against the backdrop of skyscrapers and satellite dishes.

Through Yoneda's design, the client gained not only space but the coveted connection to the outdoors. Yoneda preserved his clients' privacy by elevating the house above the level of the busy sidewalk abutting the property. A pulley at the back of the house is used to lower the garbage on collection days, and a spiral staircase serves as a connection as well as a buffer between the front door above and foot traffic below. From its top landing the clients can greet friends or call down to deliverymen without exposing the inner workings of their home.

The circular staircase slips neatly between the double-layered facade's two walls. The innermost layer, a sheet of clear glass stretched like plastic wrap across the house's first floor, keeps rain and wind out. The outer layer, a blank white wall facing the street, acts as a privacy screen. A vast improvement over the old house, where a cloth curtain was all that separated the family kitchen from the family business, the solid wall draws a clear line between private and public realms. Where the outer wall stops short, interior connects directly with exterior via natural light coming in and a carefully edited view outside. On the upper floors, the opaque wall shifts to frosted glass, serving first as the facade, then wrapping around the parapet and transitioning into the roof. The milky glass obscures views in as well as out and fills the interior with a soft light that changes throughout the day.

The most direct interface with nature is, of course, the garden itself. The client, a devoted gardener, felt deeply attached to the potted plants that stood in front of the old house, and asked Yoneda to incorporate them into his new home. Cramped site conditions meant the most logical place for planting was the roof. Though tiny, the rooftop garden contains an artful arrangement of native trees, flowering shrubs, and a stone basin for the family turtle. A quiet, contemplative retreat, separated from the main house only by a clear glass wall, the garden is also an integral part of the house.

Inside the house there are few walls or doors. Instead, level changes separate rooms and define functional zones. Habitable spaces become more private toward the top of the house, but every room opens onto the central circulation void. Even the bathroom is partitioned only by clear glass. This transparency provides muted natural light to every room and allows the cheerful sounds of children at play to resonate throughout the house. Though the division between house and city is unequivocal, borders within the house are decidedly fluid.

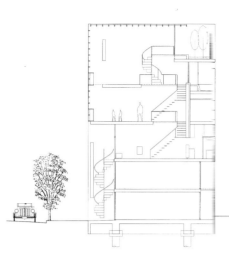

Opposite: All the rooms open onto a dramatic void space extending from the dining room to the rooftop garden.

Above left: Capping the three-story void, a glass roof fills the interior with soft, ambient light.

Above right: Longitudinal section.

Above right: A combination of spiral and straight stairs wraps the perimeter of the central void.

Overleaf: At night, Ambi-Flux glows amoung the adjacent darkened commercial buildings (left). Designed by Yoneda, a wall-mounted cabinet holds dishes and the *butsudan* Buddhist altar. A cube near the front door is for shoes (right).

"Though the division between house and city is unequivocal, borders within the house are decidedly fluid."

Ambi-Flux; Akira Yoneda / architecton Tokyo

Opposite: Cantilevered and column
free, Balcony House a street-level
commercial space, below a two-
floored residence.

Right: The band of windows in the
master bedroom captures a sprawling view of the streets below and
the hillsides beyond.

Below: Longitudinal section.

Overleaf: The living-room and din-
ing-area windows flood the space
with light and breeze and offer an
interactive view of the surrounding
neighborhood.

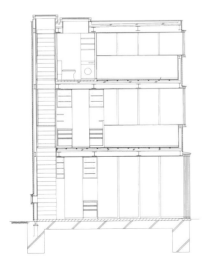

A number of years ago, architect Takaharu Tezuka was walking around London's Regent's Park when he was struck by a novel idea. Gazing at the nearby houses and their attached balconies, the architect thought to himself: What if a house was a balcony?

Tezuka and his wife, Yui, eventually tested this hypothesis when they landed a unique commission to design a combined house and dog boutique for a couple, their young son, and two canine companions. The clients, who started designing luxury leashes and collars primarily as an Internet business, decided the time had come for a shop of their own. They purchased land in Zushi, a beach community in Kanagawa Prefecture not far from Tokyo, and hired the Tezukas to design their dream house.

Occupying a corner site surrounded by nondescript apartment blocks and parking lots, the property is not beautiful. Though it is only 33 feet (10 meters) from the beach, existing buildings block any view of the sea. The Tezukas grappled with how to incorporate the waterfront when a direct visual connection was not possible. Collaborating with the architect/engineer Masahiro Ikeda, the Tezukas filled the permissible building envelope with a 30-foot-tall (9-meter-tall) building that was completed in 2001. The building is strategically placed where sun and sea breeze can flood the interior.

"The best way to catch wind, view, and customers was to make the building out of balconies," explains Tezuka. The architects sliced the blocky house into three separate but not equal levels, with varied ceiling heights reflecting a programmatic hierarchy. The ground floor is shared by the shop and café. A dog lover's paradise, the emporium not only stocks all manner of canine-themed merchandise but includes a small shower room for retrievers and a snack bar that serves tea as well as dog biscuits. The entire commercial area is paved with easy-to-hose-down concrete. The clients' living and dining areas fill the second floor, topped by a combined design studio and family bedroom above. Galley kitchens and bathrooms for residence and retail are grouped together in a utility core running up the back of the building. A metal grille staircase provides access to all levels and culminates in a transparent hatch opening onto the roof.

Each level is enclosed on three sides with wraparound glass: floor-to-ceiling doors at grade level and sliding strip windows interspersed with bands of reddish wood cladding on the two upper floors. As the building ascends, the height of the glass decreases reflecting the need for greater privacy on the upper floors. A completely permeable membrane, the first floor's movable panels can be stowed away, allowing people and their pets to move freely in and around the shop. Upstairs the windows may be pushed aside, filling the residential quarters with a rush of fresh air and framing panoramic views of distant mountains. Sailcloth awnings shield the shop, and the Tezukas' version of traditional sudare roll shades cut the afternoon glare upstairs.

"Upstairs the windows may be pushed aside, filling the residential quarters with a rush of fresh air and framing panoramic views of distant mountains."

Balcony House; Takaharu + Yui Tezuka / Tezuka Architects, Masahiro Ikeda / mias; Kanagawa Prefecture

Opposite: Blurring the boundary
between inside and out, the street,
level dog boutique and café
can be completely opened on three
sides. The café's kitchen hugs
the fourth wall.

Right: A substantial skylight admits
a generous view of the sky to the
bathroom below.

Far right: The open and inviting
ground floor embraces the square
immediately in front of the property.

At the building's base, where café tables overflow onto the surrounding property, there is no division between interior and exterior. The natural flow of light, air, and movement at grade level are responsible for the shop's pleasant, casual atmosphere. Upstairs, there s a seamless connection between interior and exterior. While 180-degree windows offer a fluent visual dialogue with the outdoors, the conspicuous absence of corner columns completely alters the way the space is perceived. "Once you remove the corner colums, nothing separates in and out," explains Takaharu Tezuka.

This strategy required structural innovations. "We wanted to get rid of columns altogether," explains Ikeda. Ultimately the designers concealed all vertical supports within the staircase and service core and the adjacent sidewalls. Together with diagonal braces, the hidden columns hold up the cantilevered floor slabs. Jutting out like giant bookshelves, each cantilever is actually a heavy, boxlike steel truss camouflaged by the facade's wood cladding. To ensure stability in an earthquake-prone region, Tezuka used trusses that were sufficiently deep but not too wide or too long.

Although the house looks unique, the path the architects took was not unknown. "We didn't actually create a new structure but found a new application for an existing system," explains Tezuka. Used routinely for gas stations and other places in need of column-free space for cars to maneuver, cantilevered beam structures are familiar sights. Still, it took time for all parties concerned to feel comfortable with this unconventional solution. "That often happens on my projects," chuckles Ikeda. "While the house was under construction, there were temporary columns in each corner," says Tezuka, "but at the end the carpenter was scared to take them out."

"While the multiple level changes lead to mazelike living areas, they also supply many opportunities to appreciate the courtyard, the actual and figurative heart of the house."

Opposite: A single tree and two elliptical disks of ground cover are the only living elements in this minimalist garden.

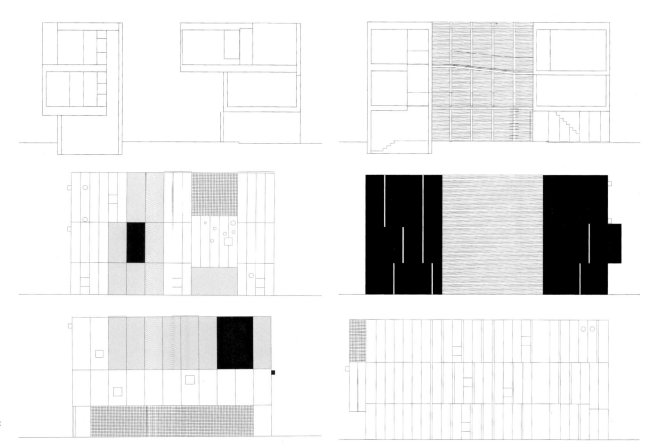

Right (clockwise from top left): Cross section; longitudinal section; north elevation; south elevation; east elevation (facade); west elevation.

Overleaf: Contained within a steel-clad box, the *tatami* room is visible above the living room. A spiral staircase leads from the *tatami* room to the roof.

Covered with asphalt parking lots, rabbit-hutch houses, and a forest of aboveground telephone poles, Tokyo suburbs bear little resemblance to the planned garden communities that were developed around American or English cities in the twentieth century. Yet somehow Fukuoka architect Hiroyuki Arima had to accommodate these typical conditions to the aspirations of a client who dreamed of "living with nature."

Though lacking scenery, the suburban neighborhood is extremely convenient by Tokyo standards. Located on a major railway line, it is an easy commute into Shibuya, one of Tokyo's many commercial hubs. The client, an information-technology businessman, wanted the option of working at home. He and his wife required an on-site office, a bedroom suite for his aging mother, and private accommodations for visiting friends.

Beyond their specific room requests, the clients left the house's overall concept up to Arima. The architect's solution was a simple cube that politely turns its back on the neighbors. Sliced into three parts, the house, which was completed in 2002, consists of two narrow blocks of living space with a generous courtyard in between. Exterior and interior corridors tie the blocks together. Shielding the rest of the house from the street, the front block contains a four-car garage and the entrance, disguised as a plain panel to blend in with the white-walled facade. The second level features a living room and kitchen, followed by two small multi-purpose rooms on the third level — one *tatami* floored where

futon can be rolled out for overnight guests. On the opposite side of the courtyard, the office — set a few steps below grade level — forms the base. The mother's suite, complete with a built-in alcove for a traditional-style Buddhist altar, is on the second floor, followed above by the master bed and bath. Grass-covered roof terraces — the only greenery in sight — cap both parts of the house.

The architect laced both halves of the structure with gaping voids and subtle level changes that break up the regularity and link floors vertically. As in traditional homes, rooms lead directly to rooms, eliminating the need for internal corridors. The entire house is bound together by a circulation loop that begins at the front door and wraps around the courtyard.

Arima integrated nine runs of stairs as well as an elevator that stands midway between the two halves, enclosed in its own semi-detached, steel-clad structure. While the multiple level changes lead to mazelike living areas, they also supply many opportunities to appreciate the courtyard, the actual and figurative heart of the house. "It's like mountain climbing," explains Arima. "You see the garden differently from different vantage points."

More restrained *ikebana* installation than lush landscape creation, the garden contains only a single *tsubaki* tree, whose delicate white flowers appear in summer and autumn, and two patches of *ryuge* "dragon's beard" ground cover that remain year round. Each element is positioned as carefully as branches in a *kenzan* flower frog. A firm believer

"Straddling the line between transparency and opacity, the exterior walls shield the house yet allow it to breathe."

Introspective House; Hiroyuki Arima; Kanagawa Prefecture

Opposite: Projecting elements, such as the elevator encased in a square steel tube and the cantilevered cubic *tatami* room with its cylindrical *tokonoma* alcove, articulate the courtyard perimeter.

Right: View toward the courtyard from the roof.

Far right: View through the second-floor lavatory.

in Mies van der Rohe's adage "Less is more," Arima explains: "It is easier to appreciate nature if there is just one tree." The house's light-limiting height precluded a full-fledged spread of greenery as well. Contrived and controlled as any traditional *tsuboniwa* courtyard, Arima's rendition is not just a visual conduit to bring light, air, and view inside; its white wood deck can comfortably accommodate large-scale entertaining.

The courtyard is far from private. Like a glass fishbowl, it is visible from nearly every part of the house, allowing the clients, as requested, to look up, down, and across at one another throughout the day. Keeping an eye on the client's mother is particularly easy since her windowed bedroom juts out into the courtyard. Because the clients reasoned that visitors might prefer a bit more enclosure, the *tatami*-floored guestroom, protruding from the opposite side, is swaddled in stainless steel. A gleaming silver box with a white cylinder at one end containing a circular *tokonoma* alcove for display, the *tatami* room bounces sunlight off its reflective surfaces.

Straddling the line between transparency and opacity, the exterior walls shield the house yet allow it to breathe. At the street, steel mesh walls enclose the garage but reveal the courtyard beyond. Up above, large glass panes flood the living room with daylight and open the house to views out. At one end, a thin skin is all that separates the clients' courtyard from a vacant lot next door. Made of black concrete panels accented with slivers of glass, the beautiful wall not only is a gift to the neighbors who pass it each day on their way to the station but also draws an explicit boundary at the edge of the house.

What will happen in the future to the adjacent land is uncertain. It is Arima's hope that his house will set a good example for subsequent development. Regardless of what rises next door, the garden respite, with its personalized view of the sky, will remain protected by its cocoonlike house.

Opposite: The roof is topped with grass complementing the limited greenery below.

Left: Though a half floor lower, the client's office is visually connected to the courtyard and the family quarters upstairs.

Below: The garage (foreground) and the office (background) on the ground floor filter out street-level activity.

"Grass-covered roof terraces — the only greenery in sight — cap both parts of the house."

Introspective House; Hiroyuki Arima; Kanagawa Prefecture

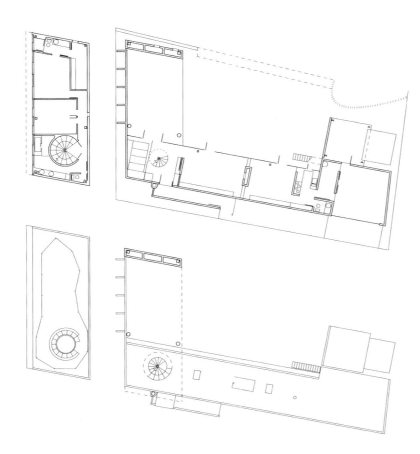

The site for S House, a 1,700-square-foot (158-square-meter) home designed by Jun Aoki, was a mixed blessing. Although the large property faces the ocean, a four-lane superhighway separates it from the seashore. To navigate around this fairly major impediment, Aoki proposed a three-story house but omitted the second floor. The ground floor hugs the ground and faces inward toward an enclosed garden, and the third floor, perched on spindly columns like the crow's nest of a ship, is high enough to look past the trucks and cars below to the waves and whitecaps beyond.

The project launched when Aoki's client returned to Odawara, a seaside community ninety minutes west of Tokyo. After living ten years in Los Angeles, he wanted to move home and help manage the family fish-sausage factory. Happy to return to the small town where he was raised, he couldn't quite leave California behind. With hopes of bringing the West east, the client went, model in hand, to Aoki. "I wanted to enjoy the ocean view. I wanted to enjoy the sunshine. And I wanted to enjoy my own yard," he explained.

Although Aoki had never lived in the United States, he and his client were like-minded. Their collaboration began by choosing a site from among the various family-owned properties in and around Odawara. They selected this plot for its potential, for its connection to the childhood memories of the client, who grew up nearby, and for its convenient location, five minutes from his office.

Facing the beach, the plot is engulfed by a densely developed residential neighborhood. Because privacy protection was a concern, "S" does not open directly onto the road, and its street presence is as restrained as any stately old home. Instead of a revealing facade, a solid masonry plane fronted by a row of windblown pine trees masks the interior. The wall, whose pebbly surface recalls indigenous *tsuchikabe* mud-wall construction, wraps the house on two sides, eliminating the view of oncoming cars, as well as the ocean. A narrow, stepping-stone path, hidden by a sea blue wall, bridges the gap between public throughfare and private threshold.

Concealed behind this anonymous barrier is an L-shaped house framing an expansive lawn, completed in 1996. A mounded earth ridge and a storeroom border the other two sides. Attached to the main house, the storage area is reminiscent of the freestanding plaster-walled *kura* storehouses traditionally built by well-to-do families to safeguard their treasures.

The house itself consists of two perpendicular single-story legs, one at ground level and one on the third floor, which overlap at the entry foyer. Though divided by subtle level changes, the ground-floor wing is essentially a single continuous space extending from the entry foyer. A tiny four-mat *tatami* room lines one side of the foyer while the other leads into the living room. Complete with fireplace, the living room is followed by the dining room and a kitchen that culminates

Opposite: Spiral stairs lead from the entry foyer to the second-floor roof terrace and the third-floor bedrooms.

Right: In the children's bedroom, Aoki lined opposite walls with built-in furnishings, preserving the option to divide the room with a center partition.

Below left: The foyer joins the living room, where sliding doors open onto the lush lawn.

Below right: Shielded by a wall, a narrow walkway leads to the front door.

"The ground floor hugs the ground and faces inward toward an enclosed garden, and the third floor, perched on spindly columns like the crow's nest of a ship, is high enough to look past the trucks and cars below to the waves and whitecaps beyond."

Opposite: Floor-to-ceiling glass separates the living room from the garden; the tile floor segues smoothly into the gridded grass lawn.

Right: Shielded from the highway by a blank wall, the double-height, covered terrace is tucked beneath the third-floor bedrooms.

Below: Longitudinal section.

Overleaf: S House soars over the neighboring tile-roofed buildings, offering its residents a glimpse of the sea.

in a service entrance and a California-style two-car garage. In contrast to this flowing sequence, the third floor was arranged as compactly as a ship's cabin. The two bedrooms — the children's lined with built-in captain's beds on either side — face the water, and the bathroom components are tucked around the spiral stairs. Access to the indoor and two rooftop outdoor spaces is granted by two sets of stairs, one exterior and one interior, that wind around each other like a double helix. Together they hold vertical levels and overlapping horizontal legs together like a giant pin joint.

In addition to their functional and organizational distinctions, the two enclosed floors engage the outdoors in two different ways: One faces the garden, and the other looks out to sea. On the ground floor, the living room's glass wall opens onto a gridded lawn. By contrast, the third floor all but turns its back on the greenery below. Oriented toward the sea, strip windows ensure ocean vistas from every room, including the shower. Double-paned glass controls unwanted noise, but vibrations from gale winds and rumbling trucks were challenging to eliminate completely. By forgoing a

second level and doubling the height of the ground-floor-level ceiling, Aoki visually and audially distanced the third-level sleeping quarters from the rush of traffic below. The resulting double-height void beneath the third floor is the perfect place for outdoor entertaining. A covered outdoor room with a ceramic tile floor, it is one of the house's many exterior spaces. The external areas are linked by an outdoor circulation loop that moves from ground-floor garden to roof terrace.

While it may be accomplished in different ways, integrating the interior and exterior is common to houses on both sides of the Pacific. Yet Aoki's negotiation of extreme site conditions was a distinctly Eastern approach. A similar site abutting a heavily trafficked highway would be difficult to sell in the United States. In Japan, where ideal situations are hard to find, architects expect adverse conditions and design around them like any other project constraint. By elevating the house, Aoki managed to steer clear of not only the roadway but also the waterfront's unsightly elements. Odawara's beaches, like much of Japan's coastline, are littered with concrete bollards and are best seen from afar.

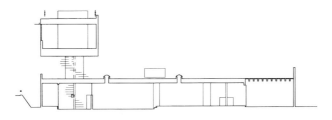

"Facing the beach, the plot is engulfed by a densely developed residential neighborhood."

Despite Japan's overall affluence and growing internationalization, many modern couples still follow the tradition of living with an extended family under one roof. Some live as a single, multigenerational family. Others build homes accommodating two, or even more, separate households. Either way, lifestyles necessarily shift. Faced with such a commission, the architect must consider ways to orchestrate widely divergent expectations while also anticipating family change.

In modern day Japan there is no social obligation to live with one's parents, but in the past there was no choice. Before World War II, Japan was largely an agrarian society based on the social unit of the *ie*, or extended family. Within this structure, family members worked the land and lived side by side. At that time, "the house rather than the individual was important." explains Tokyo architect Makoto Motokura. Leadership of the family passed from father to eldest son who was responsible for the care of his aging parents but also inherited the family homestead. In addition to the *omoya*, or main house, some properties also had a *hanare*, or small, separate house, used by either a young or an aging couple. Other siblings were free to move out and set up households of their own. Rooted in feudalism and religious tenets, this deeply entrenched system cut across all social strata, from landed gentry to lowly farmer.

Japan's defeat by the Allied powers in 1945 led to the breakdown of the extended family. Increased migration to major cities in the postwar period and the fast-paced adoption of all things Western contributed to the social shift. As the number of city-dwelling, white-collar workers grew and farmers diminished, American-style nuclear families, made up of husband, wife, and their offspring, replaced the all-inclusive *ie*. Yet this change was not purely a result of physical separation. "The freedom to choose one's line of work led to a feeling of greater independence by the younger generation," says Tokyo architect Jun Aoki. This loosening of the strict social organization naturally led to changes in living patterns and house plans.

In recent decades the definition of family or household has broadened considerably and now includes every variation from singles electing to live alone to extended, multigeneration families. "There is both a revival of *ie* and people who do not want to rely on their families," says Yoko Kinoshita. "Today both are acceptable." Currently, some larger families now are building multigenerational houses that enable them to live close enough that "the miso soup won't get cold" but with a measure of privacy and autonomy for everyone. Though concentrated in major cities like Tokyo, these houses are emerging in other parts of the country as well.

The reasons for the popularity of the new multigenerational house are both economic and social. In large cities, especially in Tokyo, many young couples cannot afford a home of their own. Property prices in Japan's capital city are beyond the means of many prospective homeowners. As a result, says architect Akira Yoneda, "Multigeneration houses are a very popular or inevitable approach." For new families, the prospect of moving in with parents or in-laws conveniently located in the city may be preferable to buying a home of their own in a suburb an hour and a half away or more.

Many extended families choose to live near one another simply because they enjoy the integration of daily routines, but often they do not want to actually reside together because of basic lifestyle differences. "It is easy if you want to see each other and easy if you don't" says one client, "but the rhythm of daily life is completely different if you live apart, and it takes effort to communicate." At the same time, families may go for a week or more without seeing each other. For many younger couples the growing need to care for aging parents is a major consideration. It is reassuring to be able to check on a relative's well-being by glancing unobtrusively out the window or catching a snippet of conversation. If a family member's health deteriorates, it is far simpler to provide care from next door than from the next town.

While medical advances have increased life expectancy in Japan significantly, elder sons — following recent social trends — feel less obligated to look after their parents. Today there is no clear-cut rule for who will watch over the elderly. "If there is no house, then the entire care system is upset," explains Motokura. While elder care facilities are beginning to proliferate countrywide, they are not a viable option for some or an appealing choice to others.

The care-giving benefit of multigenerational living is not just a one-way street; omnipresent grandparents can provide a wonderful source of built-in chic care. As more and more women enter the workforce, this service is increasingly valued. Although high-quality, government-subsidized child care is available to working mothers, it does not meet everyone's needs. Long hours and late nights are still regular conditions in the Japanese workplace, and there is no substitute for a home-cooked meal or the attention lavished by a loving grandparent.

For these reasons, many couples willingly start their married life moving in with one set of parents or building a multigenerational house together. Other families decide to share a house later on, perhaps after a parent's death. More often than not, the existing house is unfit to accommodate the divergent needs of multigenerational cohabitation. If they have the resources, many clients will keep their land but tear down and replace the old building with a new one better suited to their combined needs. Alternatively they may sell the old property and rebuild on a newly acquired parcel.

There is also no set formula for payment. Frequently the older couple supplies the land and the younger one pays for construction. Though the younger couple may one day face heavy inheritance taxes on the land, this is still a profitable arrangement. For families living in Tokyo, it is certainly more economical for multiple generations to live together on one plot than to buy adjacent apartments that can be prohibitively expensive and difficult to tailor to the inevitably changing family needs.

Freedom to expand, contract, or reconfigure the home at a later date is a high priority for most clients. "Ten years in the life of a house means so much," says architect Keiichi Irie. "During that time, the kids grow up and grandparents age, both of which require changing the interior, so a house must have spatial flexibility." With land availability at a minimum and permissible building volumes extremely restrictive, adding on to an existing house is not an option for most homeowners in Tokyo. Instead, possible future changes to the layout must be considered and incorporated from the start. Grandparents' rooms, for example, may be located where they can be assigned new functions as the family evolves. Or the plan may be designed so that walls can be removed to combine two households or added to segregate a portion of the interior. Accessibility for wheelchairs and walkers is another consideration. Even if there is no immediate need for a mini-elevator or ramp, many architects allot space for them.

By far the most pressing design issue concerns where the independent domains overlap and how to integrate different lifestyles. "The challenge is to make a relationship between the two residences," says Kinoshita. "Where the two units meet is where something interesting happens."

Separate units for different households may be stacked vertically, lined up side by side, placed end to end, or even embedded one inside the other. Clearly divided houses can lease units to unrelated tenants. Most clients want an area where they can interact with other family members. Many share an entrance, courtyard, garden, or another circulation space, while other areas, such as kitchens and sitting rooms, exist in duplicate.

Stylistically the dividing line between two generations may be clearly drawn as well. The older generation may be more conservative and tradition-bound in their selection of finishes and furnishings, choosing *tatami* over tile and *futon* over beds. Likewise, in places inhabited by an older couple, doorsills, high bathtubs, and other potential barriers may be avoided altogether. In other cases materials and details are used to unify the house and make two functionally discrete domains read as one.

Previous page: The formal Western elevation provides a secondary entrance to this warehouselike structure.

Opposite: Entrance to the grandmother's quarters.

Right: A cluster of stairs leads to private bedrooms (left), public gathering areas (right), and down to the front door.

Clad with industrial-grade black metal panels, Waro Kishi's House in Higashi-Otsu both looks and acts like a warehouse. The exterior of the house is intended to remain the same over time, but its interior accommodates change as the family inevitably shrinks or grows. Like stored goods, the house's functional pieces can be moved around to accommodate migrating family members. Kishi kept rooms as neutral as possible, making it easy for people or partitions to trade places. Though the anticipation of future changes was a central design theme, the architect's top priority was making a home where the family currently can enjoy each other's company and have plenty of private space too.

Built for a middle-aged couple, their two adult children, and the wife's mother, the house is located in a quiet residential enclave in Otsu, a small city between Kyoto and Osaka. Kishi's L-shaped building occupies a triangular site fronting a narrow, meandering road. Today the area is dotted with conventional tile-roofed homes, but when the client's father purchased the land in 1965, it was still undeveloped forest. The father promptly put up three houses that remained standing until his death, when high inheritance taxes instigated the sale of two parcels to a developer. The client's son, who saw Kishi's work in a magazine, suggested the Kyoto architect as a possible designer for the third segment of the house.

Completed in 2003, the house has an extremely complicated layout. It consists of communal spaces and four "private purpose rooms" spread out over six different levels but connected by four separate sets of stairs and 82 feet (25 meters) of corridor. "It is kind of a maze," says Kishi. "The plan itself is simple but the experience is complicated."

The first floor contains the main entrance, an indoor garage, and the grandmother's *tatami* mat apartment. A self-sufficient unit with a small garden in front, the apartment has its own entrances but also connects internally to the rest of the house. Stairs beginning at the main house's front door lead up to the parents' bedroom a half flight up. From that landing, two more staircases split off in different directions. One staircase leads to the daughter's bedroom and the living room on the second floor, where additional steps lead to the eat-in kitchen. The other staircase leads to the son's bedroom, where a white metal ladder goes up to a sun-drenched loft. The loft ends in a walk-in closet. The closet in turn opens onto a small terrace, used for drying laundry, followed by a hidden staircase back down to the kitchen. The entire family (except for the grandmother) shares a single ground-floor bathroom. In the hopes of avoiding morning congestion, Kishi created discrete, segregated areas for the toilet, bath, and sinks.

Kishi's multiple entrances, splitting stairs, and winding corridors create a distinct separation between public and private rooms. Though the doorways to the sibling's quarters are far apart, the rooms are back to back. Thanks to the house's forgiving wood-frame structure, their shared partition can be removed and the two rooms turned into a single one large enough for a couple. "It is meaningless to fix rooms," explains

Kishi. To neutralize the rooms even more, the architect chose white for almost every surface inside the house. Kishi hopes that all this complexity will guarantee future flexibility.

The "private purpose rooms" are not only isolated from each other but cut off from the outdoor environment, since windows were kept to a minimum. As a result, they are quiet, intimate retreats for individuals who want to be alone. By contrast, the public rooms are where the family gathers daily to share meals, watch television, or simply enjoy one another's company. The spacious dining room is lined with elegant appliances encased in a long white counter along one side. The focus of the room is a glass-topped table in the center surrounded by comfortable chairs. Two generous windows, one at counter level and the other a clerestory, fill the airy room with sunshine "Even in the dead of winter our spirits are lifted," says the client.

The eat-in kitchen flows easily into the living room half a level below. A change in floor level defines the two distinct functional areas, while the ceiling plane unites them into one large 33-foot-long (10-meter-long) room. This huge span was beyond the capability of the wood-frame structure, so Kishi

added two steel columns and painted them white to blend in comfortably with the space.

Smaller than the eat-in kitchen, the living room is the most open and exposed space in the house. The room overlooks the street through a large wraparound plane of glass inspired by Japanese folding screens. A second pair of glass walls looks down at the grandmother's garden, where a dogwood tree blooms in late spring.

In the past, overexposure was not a concern in Japan since most well-to-do urban houses, with the exception of *machiya* row houses, did not have facades at all, let alone large street-fronting windows. Instead, the house was set back and protected from traffic by a gated wall and garden. Kishi's house has both open space in front, with a garden on one side and gravel-covered parking on the other, and a semi-detached wall. Instead of concealing the interior, Kishi's wall exposes it. An 8-inch-thick (20-centimeter-thick) barrier, the wall defines the edge of the clients' property, but its two large openings reveal the inner workings of the house, creating an important link between public and private.

Below: The living and dining areas are separated by a level change and a freestanding wall lined with storage on the living room side.

Opposite: The dining room features generous light from the adjacent living room and the clerestory above.

"To neutralize the rooms even more, the architect chose white for almost every surface inside the house."

Opposite: The kitchen's storage alcove hovers over stairs leading down to the front door.

Top right: Ground-floor plan.

Center right: Second-floor plan.

Bottom right: Third-floor plan.

Below left: Axonometric drawing.

Overleaf: The freestanding facade physically, but not visually, separates private and public domains but leaves them visually connected.

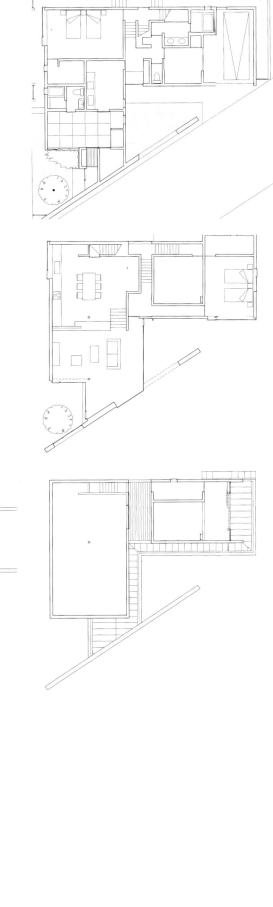

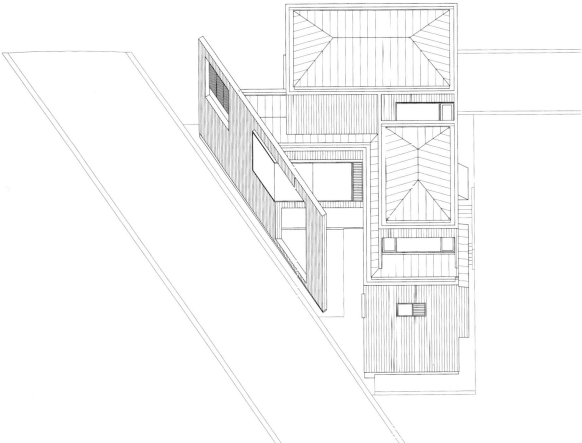

"Clad with industrial-grade black metal panels, Kishi's House in Higashi-Otsu both looks and acts like a warehouse."

"Aside from a modest entrance on one side and a pair of doors opening onto a small terrace facing the river on the other, the long thick walls are punctured only by a series of small square windows for ventilation."

Naked House; Shigeru Ban Architects; Saitama Prefecture

Japanese houses are famous for their sliding *shoji* screens and foldable *futon* beds. In Naked House, Tokyo architect Shigeru Ban took the idea a step further by making entire rooms that move. A single-story, shedlike shell, the house contains four bedroom boxes on wheels. The boxes can be freely moved from one end of the house to the other or even out onto the terrace, while the kitchen, laundry, and bathroom areas remain anchored to the perimeter walls.

Ban had been hoping to design a house with rooms that roll for some time. The trick was finding an opportunity. "I am kind of picky selecting clients, especially for houses," says Ban. "I don't want to compromise but the client shouldn't either." The client wanted a house with few closed-off, private rooms and plenty of open space where the entire family — his wife, their two young children, and his mother — could gather and enjoy each other's company. On hearing this client describe his ideal home, Ban knew he'd found a good match.

Inspired by the neighboring glass sheds, Ban wanted to build a translucent house; however, the house had to be adequately insulated, and conventional insulation tends to block out daylight. Ban's first idea was to make the exterior walls out of corrugated fiberglass sheets with shredded waste paper in between, but the paper still blocked too much light. After exploring a number of different options, Ban discovered that white polyethylene noodles used to pack fruit both let light in and kept cold out.

Although contractors in Japan can be persuaded to do amazing things, turning packing material into a wall was asking too much. Instead, Ban's staff took on the task, setting up shop in their studio, where they spent some five hundred hours spraying the noodles with fireproofing and stuffing them into transparent bags, each one quilted like a duvet to keep the noodles from settling at the bottom. The five hundred completed sacks were then carted bit by bit in the backseat of Ban's car to the site, where they were stapled to the house's structural wood frame. White nylon sheets, attached with Velcro to the wood frame, completely shield the wall contents from the habitable space and can be easily peeled off for cleaning or, says Ban, *hesokuri*, the Japanese equivalent of stashing money under the mattress.

Aside from a modest entrance on one side and a pair of doors opening onto a small terrace facing the river on the other, the long thick walls are punctured only by a series of small square windows for ventilation. The end walls, by contrast, open up completely. Louvered glass and hinged windows flood the bathroom with daylight and fresh air and sliding glass doors seamlessly connect the interior to a covered terrace. Aside from walls enclosing the bathroom and toilet, the interior is completely open, though white curtains can be pulled shut to hide the kitchen, laundry, and storage areas. White walls, ceiling, and vinyl tile floor unify the loftlike space.

This open, light-filled room is the perfect stage for Ban's movable boxes. Blurring the line between architecture and furniture, they are made of brown paper honeycomb panels held together by wood frames. Each one is a Japanese-style room on wheels, complete with *tatami* mat floors and *fusuma* sliding partitions on two sides. Independent and untethered, they can be easily maneuvered by two people within the common space and even rolled outside onto the terrace. The boxes have no climate-control devices of their own, yet it is possible to moderate their internal temperature and lighting by mooring them near one of several wall-mounted air conditioners, electrical outlets, or windows.

In contrast to the spacious communal area, the boxes are cozy and intimate. The four boxes, which belong to the couple, their two children, and the husband's mother, are the family members' private retreats. Intended for sleeping and other solitary activities, the boxes come in two sizes: 63 square feet (6 square meters) for the adults and 55 square feet (5 square meters) for the children. Both types of boxes are only big enough inside to hold a *futon*, a lamp, and a book or two. Ladders lead up to the tops of the children's boxes, where they can play or study at built-in cardboard desks. To maximize mobility and draw the family into the shared space, Ban kept the boxes as small and light as possible. Personal possessions, including clothes, are stowed in the communal storage area.

The boxes not only allow for autonomy among family members, their motility adds to the flexibility of the house overall. When the children grow up and go away to school, their boxes can simply be removed. Alternatively, the boxes may be used in combination. "If their sliding doors are taken out and they are connected linearly, the boxes become the perfect place for a Japanese funeral," laughs Ban. As its name suggests, this house was designed to satisfy basic needs. Yet its ability to expand or contract in sync with the family is a sophisticated solution to an age-old dilemma.

Opposite: Like tables and chairs, *tatami* boxes on wheels can be rearranged at whim.

Right: Everybody from grandmother to grandchild sleeps in a *tatami* box enclosed with traditional-style, opaque *fusuma* sliding doors on two sides.

Below: The kitchen (left) and bathroom (rear) are the only fixed functional areas in the house.

Below right: *Tatami* box elevations.

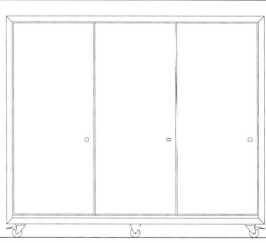

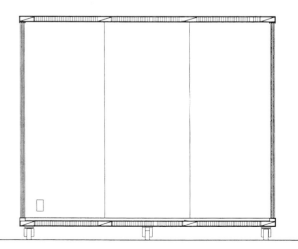

"The Tokyo-based firm designed an elegant composition of clean, concrete cubic volumes accented by warm wood doors and louvers."

tn House; ADH Architects; Tokyo

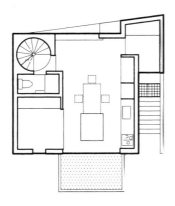
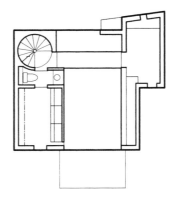
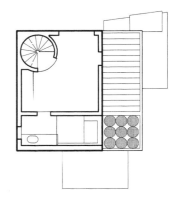
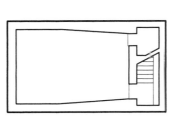
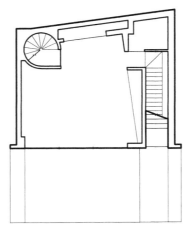
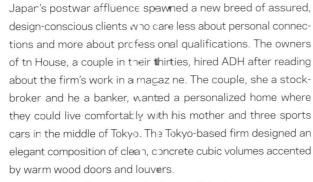

Top (clockwise from left): First-floor plan; mezzanine-floor plan; second-floor plan; ground-level floor plan; basement-floor plan

Below: Section.

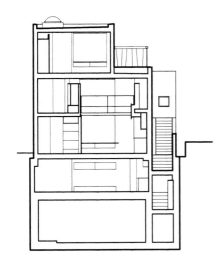

Japan's postwar affluence spawned a new breed of assured, design-conscious clients who care less about personal connections and more about professional qualifications. The owners of tn House, a couple in their thirties, hired ADH after reading about the firm's work in a magazine. The couple, she a stockbroker and he a banker, wanted a personalized home where they could live comfortably with his mother and three sports cars in the middle of Tokyo. The Tokyo-based firm designed an elegant composition of clean, concrete cubic volumes accented by warm wood doors and louvers.

Completed in 2000, the heart of the house is its combined kitchen/dining room. While the kitchen's miniscule floor area is rendered even smaller by a built-in table and island workstation in the middle of the room, its double-height ceiling makes the room feel spacious. Kitchen fixtures line one wall, opposite the mother's private quarters, and floor-to-ceiling windows feature park views that visually expand the room. In the other direction, the room flows seamlessly onto an enclosed balcony overlooking a busy two-way street.

Defined by tall wood louvered walls and extruded steel beams overhead, the balcony is an outdoor extension of the main room. Taking advantage of the central room's height, the architects inserted a mezzanine-level study and walk-in closet on either side of the core space. The couple's bed and bath are above, and below is the ground-level garage and the basement audiovisual room outfitted with state-of-the-art

screening equipment. Like a vertical corridor, a spiral staircase links the rooms that are stacked one on top of the other.

Since the couple and the banker's mother have diverse interests and lifestyles, ADH had intended to design a multigenerational home that could accommodate two autonomous apartments under one roof. "How could it be possible for two households to live in one house without stepping on each other's toes?" questioned architect Kinoshita. Those hopes were dashed by the size of the site. With a public park at the back and the front street slated for widening at some unknown date in the future, the site was surrounded by severely restrictive conditions. In preparation for the street's eventual redevelopment, the city effectively sliced a 13-foot-wide (4-meter-wide) swath off the front of the 1,076-square-foot (100-square-meter) property, reducing its buildable area to a mere 753 square feet (70 square meters). Fortunately, code variances enabled ADH to add square footage at the top and bottom of the house.

As a compromise, the architects devised a single house with two entrances: one for the couple and one primarily for the mother. The former provides direct floor access from the garage to the couple's bedroom, and the latter leads from the street to the main floor, which becomes the mother's domain when her children go to work. "Because this property is small, we had to separate private areas in section instead of plan," explains Kinoshita. Although the mezzanine level buffers the

two bedrooms and guarantees privacy for everyone, territorial lines between generations are loosely drawn and delineated in part by different schedules. The kitchen and dining area is shared, and the mother frequently prepares dinner for the family. Each individual still has his or her own personal space: the mother her bedroom, her son the screening room and garage, where he sips coffee while admiring his cars, and his wife her study, where she curls up on the *tatami* mats to study stock reports.

In many multigenerational homes, it is the grandparents who want to retain *tatami* mats and *tokonoma,* or decorative alcoves. Here it was just the opposite. The wife's study is a tiny, three-*tatami*-mat retreat accessible only by a narrow catwalk crossing the main space. The room has many characteristics of a traditional tea-ceremony room, but assembled in an untraditional way. The room's *tatami* mats lower activity to floor level, where the wife can sit at her desk, legs comfortably stowed in a *horikotatsu* trough, as she glimpses the park through a narrow slit window. *Shoji* screens can be closed to block the view or mute the sunlight.

Unlike the study, with its carefully controlled atmosphere, the couple's upstairs bedroom is a light, airy place with blond wood floors, white walls, and a picture window facing the park. For the basics of sleeping and bathing, the clients chose *futon* mattresses and a wood *ofuro* bath. Instead of overlooking a ground-level garden, the deep tub for soaking has an oblique view of the street below. The *futon* are laid out on a raised *tatami*-covered platform, making them almost as high as a bed.

By contrast, the mother's quarters are devoid of traditional references save for the sliding panel that separates it from the adjacent dining room and kitchen. Even this movable, painted wall is so understated and abstract that it blurs the line between new and old. While the intimate scale of the mother's room sets it apart from the communal kitchen, its materials and expression blend easily with the sleek lines and contemporary materials of the adjacent eating area. This compatibility comes as no surprise, since the two rooms were designed to work together.

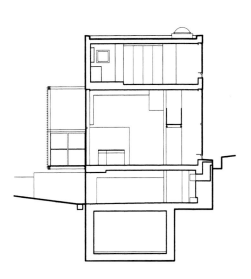

"While the kitchen's miniscule floor area is rendered even smaller by a built-in table and island workstation in the middle of the room, its double-height ceiling makes the room feel spacious."

tn House; ADH Architects; Tokyo

Opposite: The indoor vestibule and outdoor terraces at the second and third floors join the two otherwise separate households.

Having lived with her in-laws all her married life, the owner of this house might have leaped at the chance to build a home of her own. Yet when it came time to rebuild the family's forty-five-year-old homestead in Sugamo, a quiet residential neighborhood in Tokyo, no one gave serious thought to parting ways. Instead, the two couples hired architect Makoto Motokura to help them come up with a better way to continue living closely but with more privacy.

When Motokura saw the two-story wood house, his initial reaction was to tear it down and start over. The house was functionally outdated and convoluted in plan and no longer compatible with the divergent lifestyles of the three-generation family.

Completed in 1994, Motokura's new three-story concrete house is a dramatic improvement over the old one. Divided vertically, the house consists of two essentially independent dwellings: a rectilinear box for the nuclear family (the client, her research astronomer husband, and their son) and an L-shaped structure for the grandparents. The two stand side by side, connected by a common indoor entry foyer at street level leading to the grandparents' house on the left and their children's home on the right. The brilliant blue wall of the children's home creates a symbolic barrier between the two halves, and terraces on the upper floors link them back together. At grade level, both homes share a small garden extending from the elder parents' glass-enclosed living room.

Within each half, the internal workings were carefully orchestrated to balance privacy and proximity between the two households. To keep the line clearly drawn, floor levels in the two halves are the same, but programmatic pieces do not line up. Instead, they fit together like a three-dimensional puzzle. The grandparents have their kitchen and living/dining areas on the ground floor, where the younger couple sleeps. On the second floor, where the grandparents rest, their children relax in their combined living and dining room overlooking the garden. Only on the third floor, where the younger family's atelier and the older family's study join via a small terrace, do rooms functionally relate to one another. The grandson's bedroom is also on the third floor, completely beyond hearing range of his parents' private quarters two floors below, creating yet another layer of privacy within the younger family's abode.

While functional separation ensures privacy, the careful placement of walls and windows knits the two sides together, allowing voices to travel, eyes to wander, and both sides to detect activity next door even though they may go for days without direct contact. A simple, unobtrusive glance out the window is all it takes to know that all is well across the way. "We can tell just from the lighting what they are doing and whether they are up or asleep," says the daughter-in-law.

Domestic proximity also ensures a mutual support system. Having grandparents nearby who were ready and willing to look after their young grandson was a great asset that helped the daughter-in-law build her own business as a lighting designer. Today the grandson can still eat with his grandparents if his mother and father are unable to get home in time for dinner. On the other hand, should the need to look after the grandparents arise in the future, the younger family will be able to easily return the favor.

This house was expressly designed in anticipation of changing family needs. Though it consists of two discrete pieces, the house's interior space can be entirely redistributed as the family evolves. By simply enclosing the terraces the two halves can be combined into one. The unified building can then be divided horizontally, turning the ground floor into a barrier-free apartment or the top floor into a self-contained unit for the grandson or all three floors into separate dwellings. With all these options, the family expects to be able to stay in the house regardless of how they expand or contract.

The use of similar wall and window treatments on both sides will also be useful if the family decides to remodel. Neither side has *tatami* mats, but both have natural wood flooring, yet there are differences, too: The scale of the grandparents' rooms is smaller, and their functional divisions are more clearly defined, while the younger generation chose ambiguous borders and loose connections. In contrast to the grandparents' living, dining, and kitchen areas, which are comparatively dark and rooted to the ground, the younger generation's versions are light-filled and airy. A glass-enclosed, double-height, skylit space running the length of their living/dining room links it to the third floor and floods the entire floor with daylight.

When the sun goes down, the daughter-in-law's custom-designed fixtures smooth out any differences in light quality. She intentionally omitted ceiling fixtures in the grandparents' lavatory so that the room is bathed in soft light conducive to a relaxing soak in the tub. In her living room, a hidden channel of light illuminates shelves. Where the house greets the street, strips of glass running the height of the building on either side of the entrance light up at night, turning the entire house into a giant *andon* lantern. A combination of clear and frosted glass obscures inside activity but opens the house to the neighboring community.

Opposite: The scale of the two-family home harmonizes with the low-rise apartment buildings nearby.

Top left: Section.

Top right: South elevation.

Right: North elevation.

Below left: The younger generation's dining area, with kitchen beyond.

Below right: The younger generation's double-height living room showcases lighting fixtures designed by the wife.

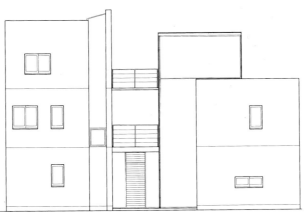

Opposite: Deliberate placement of windows and terraces establishes a sense of physical and visual connection between the two sides of Chikada House.

Right: The younger generation's combined living/dining room overlooks the garden one floor below.

Right: First-floor plan.

Far right: Second-floor plan.

Below: Third-floor plan.

"A single flat roof, a shared entry portico, and, of course, the expansive garden unite the two halves, but for the most part they behave as independent homes."

Zig / Zag; NASCA; Tokyo

Previous pages: A stone path winds through the property's lush garden to the shared entry vestibule beyond.

Opposite: A glass-covered dining table doubles as display space in the architect's dining room.

Most architects never get the chance to design for 10,764-square-foot (1,000-square-meter) residential lots in the middle of Tokyo, let alone live on one. When architect Nobuaki Furuya designed a home for himself and his parents, he got to do both. Making the decision to live together was the easy part. The house's design phase, by contrast, took five years. In the beginning, Furuya's parents had many requests and were determined to refurbish their old home. Although the construction quality of their home was lacking, his parents were very attached to the house that they built themselves in 1969. At that time, they had decided to return to the family homestead following their own period of independent living. While the structure has been altered continually, the land has remained a constant since 1935, when Furuya's grandfather began leasing the property from a wealthy landowner, as was the common practice in prewar Japan. After the war, when real estate could be purchased cheaply, the family bought it outright.

One obstacle in maintaining the original structure was orientation. The house stood in the center of the site, leaving little room for the architect to build an addition. Another constraint was the desire to preserve the site's existing garden, a vibrant array of flowering bushes and fruit-bearing trees. Even the local city government had a say, granting three trees special protection status and offering compensation to the family for saving an existing hedge instead of replacing it with a wall. At one time large plots and big houses were commonplace in this neighborhood; but the economic lure of development spurred many property owners to divide their land into small pieces or fill it with apartment blocks, usually at the expense of trees and greenery.

Furya's parents ultimately consented to rebuild altogether. The new structure consists of two L-shaped pieces arranged end to end: "Zig" for Furuya's parents and "Zag" for the architect, his wife, and their two teenage children. A single flat roof, a shared entry portico and, of course, the expansive garden unite the two halves, but for the most part they behave as independent homes.

The building process occurred in two stages. The first stage, Zig, was completed in 2000. The house contains a living and dining room, kitchen, and tatami-floored bedroom, as well as storage, bath, and lavatory on the first floor. The second floor contains an art studio, sitting room, and guestroom suite. The second stage, Zag, was finished in 2001. Like its twin, Zag contains a combined living/dining room, kitchen, bedroom, bath, and storage on the first floor, but children's bedrooms, a study, and an atelier fill the second floor.

Although the two plans practically mirror each other on paper, the actual rooms are quite different in their finishes, furniture, and floor levels. Programmatic constraints and privacy concerns led Furuya to reverse ceiling heights on either side of the entry portico. Where Zig's living-room ceiling is low, Zag's soars to 10 feet (3.2 meters). Upstairs, Furuya's mother, an artist with an appetite for big canvases and bold brushstrokes, had to have a high-ceilinged atelier, while Furuya and his wife chose more intimately scaled rooms. Staggered ceiling heights, of course, create staggered floor levels. Together they divert sight lines and help maintain a healthy separation between households.

To mediate between Zig and Zag's clean, rectangular rooms and the site's irregular outline, Furuya wrapped the narrow building with a single-story skirt that fans out toward the property's edge. Here he stuffed functional bits and pieces like his parents' fantastic collection of chests and armoires filled with decades of possessions, a small ceramics studio for his wife, and bathrooms for both households. Zig's wooden tub looks up at a skylight view of a majestic ginkgo tree and Zag's elegant limestone bath, the handmade product of a gardener who routinely carves decorative basins and other outdoor fixtures, faces a picture window looking out at the rear garden. The careful placement of glass renders the public parking lot beyond practically invisible.

In Japan, the intermingling of house and garden is very familiar, but Furuya's version is more tree house than traditional home. The approach to both halves weaves from street to stoops through the garden along a stone path. Upon crossing either threshold, visitors enter abruptly into a living room where outdoor shoes are exchanged for slippers. Instead of the typical genkan entry hall buffering the private interior from its public surroundings, the garden's bamboo barrier and curving walkway serve a transitional purpose. Though passersby may visually enjoy the garden, it is in fact the start of the family's personal domain.

The house's highly transparent exterior skin further embraces the garden's lush environs. Floor-to-ceiling strips of glass open nearly every room to expansive but vertically oriented views. Interspersed between cement panels, these windows transform interior spaces into garden observatories. Zag's dining area features sliding doors covered with mirrors to ensure a garden view for everyone seated at the table. This is a clear departure from the traditional low windows designed to frame select scenes for the benefit of those sitting on a tatami floor. "Those low windows meant that we could not walk around," explains Furuya, "just move our eyes."

Though the placement of windows diverges from historical precedent, the engineered wood structural frame recalls the substantial columns and beams found in many traditional homes. A curious blend of old and new, Zig's tatami-floored bedroom embraces convention with a contemporary edge. Though the room features traditional flourishes — fusuma sliding panels, a tokonoma decorative alcove, and an engawa-inspired porch — the presentation veers from stan-

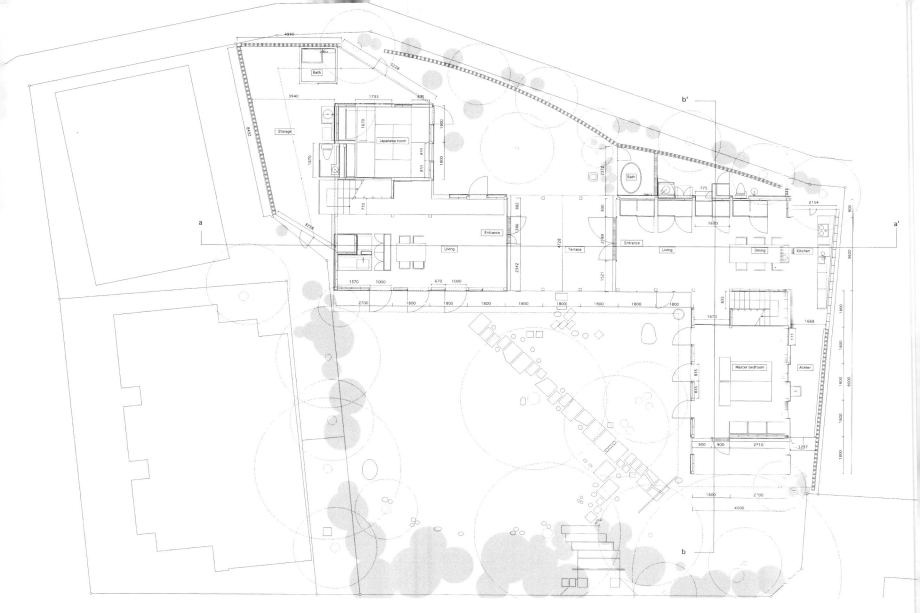

Labels in plan: 4990, Bath, 5228, 3940, 1735, 835, b', 1670, Storage, Japanese room, 1800, 8432, 1800, 835, 835, 2372, Bath, 775, 2424, 2154, 3258, a, 1670, 882, 900, 2989, 1670, 900, a', 3258, 770, 386, Entrance, Living, 4728, Terrace, 2342, Entrance, Living, Dining, Kitchen, 1570, 1000, 670, 1000, 2700, 1800, 1800, 1800, 1800, 1800, 1800, 1800, 1800, 835, 1670, 1668, Master bedroom, Atelier, 835, 835, 9500, 900, 900, 2910, 1237, 1800, 2700, 1800, b, 4500

Opposite: In the parents' home, the traditional wood bathtub is partitioned off by translucent walls, while the sink is exposed, illuminated by a skylight overhead.

Above: Site plan.

Overleaf: The covered entry foyer leads to the architect's home on the right and his parents' residence on the left (left). From her second-floor painting studio, the architect's mother can look down into her son's living room (right).

dard form: The *fusuma* are made of polycarbonate sheets, the *tokonoma* is a false front for a bank of shelves, and the *engawa* porch overlooks the living room, not the garden.

Belonging to the younger household, Zag embodies more traditional sensibilities. While *tatami* floors and *fusuma* wall panels are conspicuously absent, the entire house was planned and built according to the *tatami* mat module — a common construction practice in Japan, where many houses, even those designed by architects, are composed from stock items with standard measurements. Hallway widths and room

sizes were also determined by the prevailing *tatami* module's proportional system. This not only eased the construction process, it yielded familiar room shapes and sizes. Even the custom-designed dining table, a shallow wood drawer covered by a 9.8-foot-long (3-meter-long) sheet of glass, can be used to display everything from drawings to daisies depending on who is coming to dinner. "I designed this table because we don't have a *tokonoma* alcove in this space," explains Furuya. Traditional idioms may be gone, but the habits and customs they spawned are alive and well.

"Though the placement of windows diverges from historical precedent, the engineered wood structural frame recalls the substantial columns and beams found in many traditional homes."

Zig / Zag; NASCA; Tokyo

While living and working under one roof is not unique to Japan, such a lifestyle has enjoyed both a long history and a recent rise in popularity. Economical and efficient, the combined dwelling and workplace not only has withstood the test of the country's evolving social and geographic patterns but is flourishing as more and more individuals work out of their homes.

A traditional *magariya*-style farmhouse.

A typical *gassho-zukuri* farmhouse.

In 1603, when Edo became the capital of Japan, Tokugawa Ieyasu, the first shogun, reorganized the city around the castle and designated substantial properties as estates for samurai feudal lords. The installation of the samurai and their extensive households led, in turn, to a migration of merchants and craftsmen who worked out of their homes supplying goods and services to the ruling class. These homes, where the shop or work area usually occupied the front of the house and the living space the back, were mostly restricted to two stories because of a shogunate edict intended to keep everyone in their proper social class. These simple Edo-period (1600–1868) houses were conceptual precursors to the contemporary *tempo-tsuki jutaku*, or combined shop and home.

A different version of the shopkeeper's home, the *machiya*, developed in Kyoto. Nicknamed *unagi no nedoko*, or "eel's bedroom," *machiya* were usually long and narrow. The family business occupied the house's front room, the first in a long string of rooms connected by a corridor on one side and interspersed with a tiny garden or two to let in light and ventilation. Enclosed on either side by walls shared by neighbors, each building belonged to a large block of houses occupied by craftsmen of the same trade, such as weavers or dyers.

In contemporary Japan's tolerant architectural environment, property owners are combining private homes with various public work functions ranging from clinics and shops that depend on consumer contact to offices or studios where strangers seldom venture. The practice, far from new, has continued to evolve over the past decade. The recent surge in the freelance workforce has spawned the *soho*, or small office–home office. Likewise, a push for the decentralization of Tokyo together with the growth and development of the Internet, have led to a boom in what architect Yoshiharu Tsukamoto terms the "satellite house." These homeowners are able to live far from the urban turmoil yet maintain work affiliations via computer and occasional forays to the city.

Combined-function homes are a deeply rooted, integral part of Japanese cities, towns, and villages. In the country, family-run businesses attached to family homes have always been common, especially among farmers, for whom tending crops and animals is as much a way of life as a line of work. Throughout the ages, agricultural industries and regional climates spawned different types of *minka* rural houses, such as the *gassho-zukuri*, whose steeply gabled roof was supported by an elaborate framework that doubled as storage

for trays of silkworms in various stages of cultivation. Meanwhile, in Tohoku and other cold parts of the country, the L-shaped *magariya*-style farmhouse enabled man and beast, each inhabiting one leg of the 'L', to share their warmth. Economical and convenient, multifunction homes made sense in rural Japan.

For similar reasons, the combined home and workplace developed in urban areas as well. "The traditional neighborhood had to include services needed to maintain daily life," explains architect Yoko Kinoshita. For the small craftsman or merchant, living behind, above, or next to the shop made great sense. It eliminated the need for acquiring a second property and helped build trusting relationships with customers.

Today, station hubs, each one a node in the country's vast network of subways, buses, and trains, are the organizational element of many urban, suburban, and even exurban neighborhoods. Although major shopping districts are often just a few stops away, dry cleaners, pharmacists, florists, and other shops still serve the community according to cultural precedent. These small businesses, many of whose owners live above or behind their shops, double as gathering places whose counters and cash registers are places to exchange neighborhood news and gossip.

The proportion of commercial ventures decreases farther from the station, but no neighborhood is completely free of them. Even in Tokyo's First Class Residential Districts, the city's most restrictive zoning category, ten different types of buildings are permitted, including shops, clinics, places of worship, company dormitories, and public baths. This sweeping range is not limited to freestanding buildings. Houses combined with shops, medical clinics, restaurants, specialized schools, craftsmen's workshops, and artists' studios are often near or next to luxury homes. The only caveat is compliance with the zoning code's square-footage restrictions intended to limit the size of the commercial element.

The design of the combination home and workplace has never been the particular purvey of architects; in fact, most are designed and built by small construction companies. Recently more of these commissions have landed on architects' drawing boards because of the increase in work-at-home editors and artists, some of whom are seeking homes designed to fit their highly personalized styles of living and working.

In considering design, the architect must first address how much street exposure the family business requires. To maximize its public presence, a shop may fill the front or entire first floor, but an artist's studio or editor's office may be embedded in the house, where it has no direct connection to the street. Between these two extremes lie the doctors' offices, dental clinics, and other work venues that require easy access from the outside but do not depend on walk-in traffic.

The nature of the business determines the placement of home and office entrances. A freelancer's studio may not have an exterior door independent of the home's front stoop. A display window or shelves of merchandise may obscure the entrance to the home, itself just a curtain or sliding door at the rear of the shop. In other instances, such as when an office or consulting room is positioned side by side with the residence, the two entrances may receive equal treatment.

Within the house, the most interesting design considerations are the transition point and the overlap between home and business. Today, gradations of contact from complete independence to complete congruence exist. In some homes, the two places share nothing other than the roof; more often than not, they have some feature in common, such as a shared entry foyer. A single space may serve dual functions during the day and night: dwelling and work area. Many shops and restaurants become extensions of the family quarters once the welcoming *noren* banner is taken down for the day. Even if the dwelling has a designated study or studio, it is not uncommon for independent writers and designers to end up working in different spaces around the house.

While a staircase, space-defining corridor, or darkroom explicitly separates the two realms, more often than not the transition is unclear. In many homes a curtain, sliding *fusuma* wall panels, or a hinged, Western-style door, coupled with the traditional level change, draws the line between the public shop and the private sitting room but fails to yield an airtight separation. On the contrary, customers can hear food sizzling or dishes clattering as they retrieve shoes from the shoemaker or buy a basket of tomatoes. For the store owner, relinquishing privacy is a small price to pay for the comfort of being able to make dinner and mind the shop at the same time.

Previous page: Though architects rarely design vegetable shops, Yoko Inoue's expertise helped her clients make the most of their tiny footprint by building as tall as the building code would permit.

Left: Light floods the glass-encased stairwell.

Below (clockwise from top left): Ground-floor plan; second-floor plan; third-floor plan; elevation; sixth-floor plan; fifth-floor plan; fourth-floor plan.

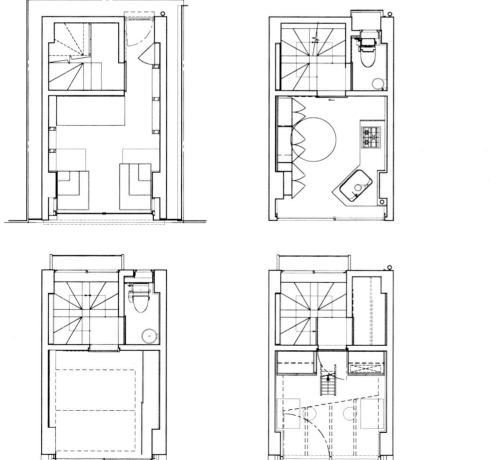

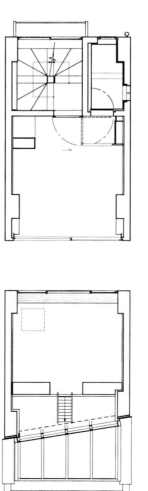

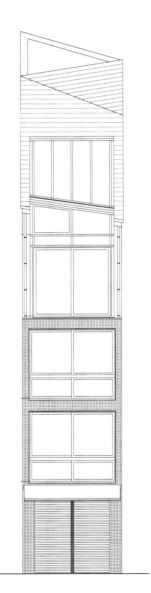

In Shinbashi, a commercial area dating from the nineteenth century, many shopkeepers sold their property during the bubble period when Tokyo land values hit their peak. Architect Yoko Inoue's clients, a third-generation vegetable seller, his wife, and three children, decided to stay and rebuild their two-story home and shop from the Taisho period (1912-26). Trying to fit more house onto their tiny plot, however, seemed almost impossible

The property, enclosed on three sides by neighboring buildings and on the fourth by the street, left little room for expansion. The rear of the site was so congested that the eaves of the existing house's roof actually dovetailed with its neighbor's, and Inoue had to shorten the original footprint by 12 inches (30 centimeters). Consequently, she had no choice but to make the building as tall as possible. While the city's precise shadow restrictions limited the house's height, Inoue still managed to replace the house and shop with a six-story "pencil building" completed n 2001.

The first programmatic piece Inoue put in place was the 140-square-foot (13-square-meter) vegetable shop facing the street. The only spot for the stairs was along the building's south side — an area traditionally designated for the most important room. As a compromise, Inoue used the staircase as a conduit for natural light by enclosing it in as much glass as possible on one side and opening it up to every major room on the other. "I wanted the stairwell to feel like a sun-room," explains the architect.

Making the most of the site's small dimensions — only 16 feet (5 meters) from front to back — Inoue filled each floor with a single room and strung them together with the staircase that acts like a vertical corridor. The second floor holds the eat-in kitchen and toilet, the third the living room and bath, the fourth the master bedroom and toilet, and the fifth a study for the two older children, who sleep in the sixth-floor loft. To optimize interior space, the architect eliminated finish materials and made structural columns and beams as deep as possible — reducing their bulky width.

Though the house is entered on the ground floor, it has no front door per se. Instead, the entire first-floor facade is completely open to the street so passersby can peruse the fresh produce and sellers can banter with their customers. Past the crates of *daikon* radishes and *kaki* persimmons, tiled shelves stocked with canned goods, and refrigerated cases is the entrance to the family home.

The transition between shop and home is rather abrupt. A narrow stairway, blocked by a retractable gate to keep the dog in and, perhaps, uninvited visitors out, is the thread connecting the two worlds. At its base, shoes are exchanged for slippers; as the staircase winds around, it widens and is lined with storage wherever possible. Inoue hollowed out walls and mounted shelves to create space for dishes, books, and other items used daily. Metal rods spanning the windows let the family dry their laundry in the sun, like everyone else in Japan.

Opposite: Though only inches deep, shelves carved out of the concrete stair enclosure add much-needed storage space.

Right: Small even by Japanese standards, the bathtub was custom-built to fit into its appointed space.

Below: Site plan.

Overleaf: The top of the house is slanted in compliance with the sunshine laws that limit the amount of shadow a building may cast on its surroundings. The glass wall invites plenty of natural light into the space.

If family members desire more privacy, they can shut the sliding partitions separating rooms and the staircase. On the street side, floor-to-ceiling glass opens the interior to unimpeded views. During the day, the children are at school, the parents are minding the shop, and glare blocks prying eyes from peering inside. When the family gathers in the evening, the house is lit up, and all its inner workings are revealed.

Within the house, privacy and personal space are difficult to come by. The parents share their bed — which fills their entire room — with their youngest daughter. The two older children, a boy and a girl, study and sleep side by side upstairs. When the youngest daughter is ready to sleep on her own, the girls will move into their own bedroom, leaving the sleeping loft all to the son and the master bedroom to the parents. This alteration will eliminate the living room — a luxury few Tokyo houses enjoy — and establish the eat-in kitchen or dining area as the communal gathering spot.

The centerpiece of this house's kitchen is its circular wood table, positioned well within an arm's length of the stove, cabinets, and counter. As compact and carefully laid out as a ship's galley, the kitchen's work area consists of a row of appliances joined by the bare minimum of counter space. The end of the counter ever had to be bent forty-five degrees to accomodate the sink. Inoue took advantage of the angled counter by loading it with storage on one side and a built-in rice bin on the other. Though she covered every available spot with shelves and cabinets, the kitchen does not feel cramped, just efficient.

Because of spatial constraints, the bathroom's fixtures — two toilets, two sinks, and one bathtub — were distributed over several floors. The spot allotted for the bath was so small that a conventional tub would not fit, so Inoue built a miniature, tile-covered version. Distributing the fixtures around the house conserved space and enabled the family to use them simultaneously.

"On the street side, floor-to-ceiling glass opens the interior to unimpeded views."

Opposite: Healtecture K's dramatic
steel wrapper encloses the client's
acupuncture clinic and herbal-
medicine shop on the ground floor
and side-by-side homes for the
client and his son above.

Right: Telescoping two layers of
corrugated steel with different
profiles enables daylight to filter
back to the parents' bedroom.
The doorway on the right connects
to a tiny terrace.

Built for an acupuncture practitioner and his family in 1996, Shuhei Endo's Healtecture K features a unique combination of clinic and pharmacy on the ground floor and two residences — one for the practitioner and his wife and the other for their son — on the upstairs levels. Located in a low-scale, residential enclave twenty-five minutes by train from central Osaka, this unusual house, wrapped with strips of galvanized steel like a traditional Japanese *furoshiki* cloth gift cover, stands slightly back from the neighboring houses. Starting at grade level, the steel rises up dramatically to form one side of the building and then bends over to become the roof. The exterior is composed of individual glass plates, though it appears as a continuous surface. Together the plates bind the building's disparate pieces together, eliminating the need for drains, as rainwater simply runs off. While the metal enclosure's dynamic profile is very eye-catching, Endo concedes that it has no particular meaning. "It was a way to wrap the spaces the client requested. If he had asked for something else the shape would undoubtedly have been different," he explains.

In contrast to the impervious metal shell, the facade is almost completely transparent. Composed of large glass panes secured by a wood-covered steel frame, the window wall takes full advantage of the building's southern exposure and visually opens the ground-floor clinic to the community — an important consideration, as the practice draws most of its patients from the surrounding neighborhood. Endo supplied full-length curtains for privacy; but most of the day the interior is visible from the street, a typically narrow lane just 16 feet (5 meters) from the front door. Though apparently narrow, the setback readily accommodates parking for two cars.

The building is easy not only to see into but to enter as well. On the first floor, are three points of entry. One door leads to the clinic — a space containing one consulting room and one four-bed treatment area. Another door opens into a pharmacy for Chinese medicines. Though the building code required separate entrances for the two public facilities, an internal door connects them.

The third entrance leads directly upstairs via a spiral staircase to the doctor's second-floor rest area, the entrance to the son's home, and more stairs up to the client's residence. Side by side but staggered in section, the two houses overlap at the third floor, where they could be connected in the future. One unit occupies the third and fourth floors of one half of the house, while the other fills the second and double-height third floor on the opposite side.

The client's house is slightly larger than that of his son. His son's unit has its own internal stairway joining the combined kitchen and living/dining room on the second floor with the bedroom on the third. Though separated by a wall, the son's bedroom aligns with his parents' combined kitchen,

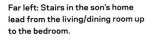

Far left: Stairs in the son's home lead from the living/dining room up to the bedroom.

Left: A short walk connects the off-street parking area in front of the building to the clinic entrance or stairs up to the two homes.

Overleaf: Despite its irregular geometry, Healtecture K coexists amiably with the conventional rectilinear buildings surrounding it on three sides.

Opposite: Warm wood mullions contrast with the corrugated-metal enclosure.

Below (clockwise from top left): Section; section; section; south elevation.

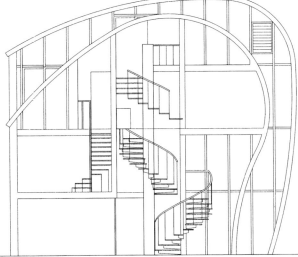

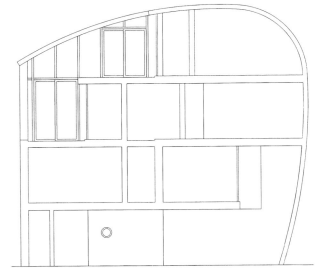

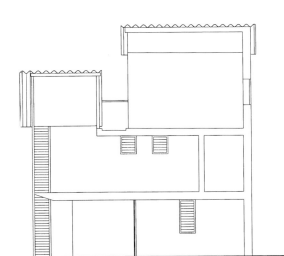

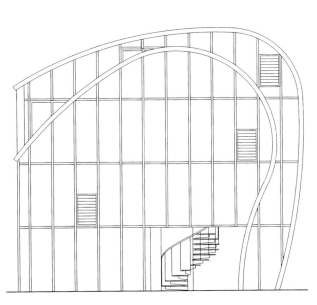

"Starting at grade level, the steel rises up dramatically to form one side of the building and then bencs over to become the roof."

Healtecture K; Shuhei Endo Architect Institute; Osaka Prefecture

Opposite: The wall near the base of the stairs leading from the doctor's rest area to his living/dining room one floor up can be removed to merge the two homes should the need arise in the future.

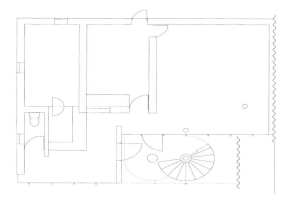
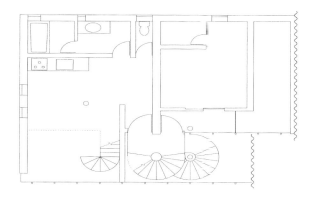
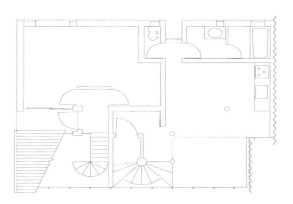
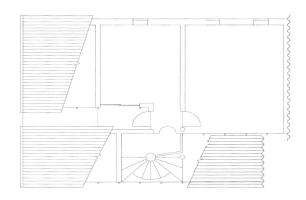

Right (clockwise from top left): Ground-floor plan; second-floor plan; fourth-floor plan; third-floor plan.

Below right: The arched floor-to-ceiling glass wall bathes the fourth-floor room in sunlight.

dining, and living area. On the parents' side, the rooms with greatest privacy upstairs on the fourth floor. Placing the most private rooms toward the rear of the house — bathrooms behind kitchens and bedrooms set back from the facade — enabled Endo to shield them from view without compromising the building's overall openness.

While the building's irregular geometry had little impact on the plan (all of the rooms are easy-to-furnish rectangles), Endo exploited its curves and soaring height as much as possible in section. Though the steel sheets were insulated to prevent the interior from becoming too hot, the architect did not allow the wood cladding or the masonry walls that divide the space in plan to mask or detract from the sloping surfaces and graceful arches of the outer shell. Instead, double-height spaces emphasize verticality and link the levels together.

In contrast to the interconnected rooms and floors within the residences, home and office are quite independent. Since the level change draws a clear line between the two environments, the structures share only an external entry precinct. The building's overall form ties the two spaces together, presenting a unified front to passersby.

Opposite: The door on the left leads to the family's second- and third-floor residence, while the door on the right leads to the father's graphic design company occupying the basement and first floor.

Right: The narrow circulation passageway holds a discreet stair-case leading from home to office.

Koh Kitayama designed this house for a Tokyo-based industrial designer who spent his childhood in Fukui Prefecture living in a combined home and food store. Though the client's decision to incorporate home and office in this new structure was in part recollective, economic and pragmatic reasoning also informed this design. By combining home and studio, the client could both save money and optimize his time with his family.

Although proximity to family was a priority, the client still wanted to draw a clear line between work and play. Koh Kitayama worked to find the ideal balance. "I wanted to come up with a new building type that is neither house nor office," says the architect. Kitayama's solution, Plane + House, was completed in 2000. In contrast to traditional antecedents where the division between shop and home was often ambiguous, there is no overlap between home and office in Plane + House. Even the entrances to the home and to the office are completely separate. The resulting structure comprises two completely independent realms stacked on top of each other. The office occupies the basement and ground floors, where employees as well as clients can come and go freely without disrupting family routines, while the upstairs houses second-floor living, dining, and kitchen areas. Sleeping quarters fill the third floor, with a loft one level above.

The separate units are bound together by a 37-inch-wide (95-centimeter-wide), skylit space that wraps the square building perimeter from top to bottom on all four sides. The width of this space was determined by the placement of the foundations. Since neighboring homes border either side of the 893-square-foot (83-square-meter) property, the foundations were pulled in from the edge of the site to ease construction. Aside from being the children's favorite place to play, the narrow space is the designated circulation zone, where people both enter the building and move between its floors. Within it, separate stairs lead up to the home in one direction and down to the office in the other. In addition, light, air, and sound travel within this band.

Circular, louvered windows in the building's inner fiber-glass skin supply all major rooms with ample muted daylight, and warm air from the ground-level office's heated floor wafts up into the residential areas. At the building front, where there are no stairs and the space is completely open, the facade's adjustable louvered aluminum panels act like a chimney that lets hot air out and cool air in. Should the summer heat become too oppressive, the clients can rely on their air-conditioning system. Even though the outer skin is a mere 21 inches (60 millimeters) thick, there was no need for insulation, since the air layer surrounding the habitable space is the best possible heat-retaining blanket.

Fixed partitions and doors are kept to a minimum. As in traditional *tatami* rooms, flexible space occupies each level, complete with *tatami* mats and sliding wood doors on the third floor. A matrix of white structural steel a contemporary

Above: Kitayama's slender steel framework modifies the traditional post-and-beam structure.

Far left: Front elevation.

Left: Section.

Bottom (left to right): Ground-floor plan; first-floor plan; second-floor plan; third-floor plan.

Opposite: The office's open-plan can be reconfigured per the client's wishes.

Overleaf: Though the house's plan is a traditional square divided into quadrants by the ceiling beams, its exposed steel structure and industrial-grade materials are strictly contemporary.

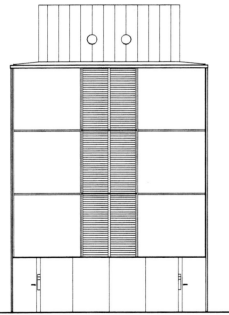

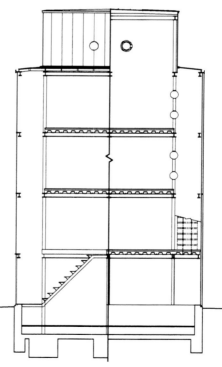

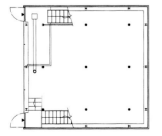
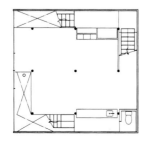

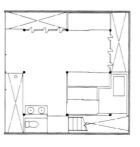

"Exposed steel floor deck and structural cross braces articulate walls and ceilings."

"A matrix of white, structural steel, a contemporary version of traditional post-and-beam construction, loosely divides the space."

Opposite: Located in a typically congested central Tokyo neighborhood, the house is set back from the street to make room for off-street parking.

Right: A four-story void topped by skylights wraps the building's square core of habitable area. Its internal walls are punctured with round windows to facilitate airflow and admit light (left). Narrow stairs wind within this circulation space, leading to the house and office (right).

version of traditional post-and-beam construction, loosely divides the space. Though partly below grade, the office is an airy environment unfettered by bulky furniture and fixed partitions. In the future, this flexibility will enable the family to adapt the house to their changing needs or even adjust the division of space between home and office.

Finished materials in both home and office were also kept to a minimum. Exposed steel floor deck and structural cross braces articulate walls and ceilings. The nine structural columns, each a mere 4 inches (114 millimeters) in diameter, are human-scaled and furniture-like. Though trendy furnishings and expensive wall treatments are conspicuously absent, the industrial image was not intended to be a neutral backdrop. It reflects the perfect marriage of the client's dislike of cosmetic decoration and Kitayama's dislike of status-laden "living fetishism," such as the unwritten rules requiring a living room to have a sofa, a coffee table, and a pendant light fixture.

The minimalist treatment makes both office and home seem informal and relaxed. Books, toys, dishes, a mechanical pet dog, and other objects of daily life mitigate whatever cold surfaces or hard edges may remain.

Opposite: Train tracks sharply define the property line at the rear of this house, belonging to an *ikebana* artist. His studio forms the central space of the tripartite building.

An *ikebana* artist of the Ryusei school, the owner of this Hiroshi Nakao-designed house is a practitioner of one of the most avant-garde branches of flower arranging. Instead of limiting his palette to flowers, he works with nearly anything that comes out of the ground. Both *ikebana* and sculpture, his *Rock 'n Roll Radish Tower*, installed in a department-store gallery, was a room-high pyramid of *daikon* radishes secured by strips of gauze. In a similar vein, Hiroshi Nakao's house blurs the boundary between art and architecture "Making this house was like making a big work of my own," explains the client. In Hiroshi Nakao, an architect who makes sculpture and a sculptor who makes buildings, the *ikebana* artist indeed found a kindred spirit.

The client encountered Nakao's work while creating an *ikebana* installation for Weekend House, the architect's first realized building. Built of black wood, the house has a primitive and slightly unsettling darkness. These qualities struck a chord with the flower arranger, and he subsequently hired Nakao to design a replacement for his family's house in suburban Tokyo. By engaging Nakao, the client saw an opportunity to make as profound an impression with his house as he does with his art. The two-story house was completed in 1996. Symmetrical in plan, it centers around its *chanoma,* or multifunctional sitting room, on the first floor and the studio on the second. The two center rooms are flanked by subsidiary spaces: kitchen, bath, and bedrooms on the first floor and additional bedrooms upstairs.

Located in a dense area, the site is hemmed in by neighboring homes, a narrow street in front, and train tracks that cut diagonally at the rear. Any hope of using black wood exterior walls was quickly dashed by the local building code. Nakao opted instead for Core-ten steel. Like a flower arrangement, the steel cladding has an organic life cycle of its own. Though they started out black during construction, the steel sheets corroded and became rust-covered after two weeks of exposure. Nakao anticipates that over time the reddish-brown surface will wear away and return to black. Though its beauty may be lost on the painting companies who routinely offer to resurface the house, the rust-covered facade has the look of lush velvet.

The interior features a long, skinny *chanoma* where the family socializes and dines. The walls, floor, and ceiling of this space are covered with structural plywood stained black. The surrounding bedrooms, bath, and kitchen — also made of black wood — flow directly into the *chanoma,* although they can be closed off with sliding partitions.

The square alcove at the far end of the *chanoma* contains a blond *tatami* mat floor and full-height glass doors that let in a burst of light, relieving the otherwise entirely black room. The small alcove one step up from the *chanoma*'s

wooden floor creates a strong sense of perspective while buffering the room from the trains outside. "I didn't really think about the use of the *tatami* room beyond its visual function," says Nakao, "But actually it is used a lot," — especially by the client, who often naps in the cozy nook.

Though very common in the West, the house's symmetrical layout is a rarity in Japan, where balance and harmony are achieved through odd numbers and irregular outlines. Intended to bring light in from two sides, Nakao's three-part plan is anything but static. Despite similarities, the two floors are also different. The first floor is horizontal and hugs the ground, but the second is vertical and oriented upward. Downstairs, where the ceiling height is low, a long, built-in glass tabletop, with a troughlike *horikotatsu* for fitting one's feet, pulls the center of activity down to the floor and marks the room's central axis.

Upstairs in the studio — the architectural heart of the house — the ceiling soars to 18 feet (5.4 meters). A ring of clerestory windows washes the dark walls with daylight and opens the room to sky views in almost every direction. A ladder in the middle of the studio leads up to a bridge connecting the roof terraces on either side, and a small square hole in the floor is a direct link to the *chanoma* below. On the studio's fixed sidewalls Nakao mounted a series of ledges to hold and display the tools of the flower arranger's trade. At one end, large panes of glass open onto a terrace and distant views of fireworks held at Tokyo Dome. At the other is Nakao's interpretation of a traditional *tokonoma* decorative shelf. "Usually *tokonoma* in Japanese houses are impossible to use," says the client. But because it is unusually deep and high off the floor, this one is very accessible, especially for this client, who prefers to look at *ikebana* from a standing position.

Another unusual feature of this *tokonoma* is its picture window. Instead of the customary blank backdrop for hanging scroll paintings, this *tokonoma* is backed by a view of the ever-changing scene outside. Situated in the center of the facade, directly above the front door, the generous square window hints at the workplace inside. While the facade appears as a single plane of steel, punctuated only by two square windows and the recessed entrance, the rear of the building is an assemblage of projecting and receding boxes. Front and back share a symmetrical, tripartite composition that steps up in the middle, corresponding to the double-height studio within. Because the client completely integrates home and work, there was no need for a separate work entrance.

Though it is difficult to divorce Nakao's body of work from the image of death — one famous installation was coffin-shaped, and another was made from discarded furnishings from an old elementary school building about

Opposite: A ladder leads up from the studio to a narrow bridge connecting roof terraces on either side.

Top: The *chanoma*, or all-purpose sitting room for the family, runs the length of the house. This picture window illuminates the black wood room, extending the sight line to the train tracks outside.

Below right: A long glass table with a *horikotatsu* foot trough below defines the room's spine.

to be torn down — this black house is not intended to be frightening or ominous. The structure has the familiar quality of a primitive, ritual space, such as in a traditional temple, where shadows abound and bright light does not belong. This atmosphere may seem counterintuitive in a house laden with practical concerns, but in fact it melds well with the client's temperament. "If I make a very strange house, perhaps it will inspire the person living in this house to make something special," says the architect.

Opposite: A band of windows in the studio provides a connection to the sky. A small opening in the floor resembling a well is a direct link to the *chanoma* one floor below.

Right: In a second-floor bedroom a small square opening is for ventilation, while a large window at one end offers a view toward the train tracks and beyond.

Below (from top): Section; second-floor plan; first-floor plan.

Overleaf: From the studio contained within the house's tallest volume, the building steps down toward the train tracks.

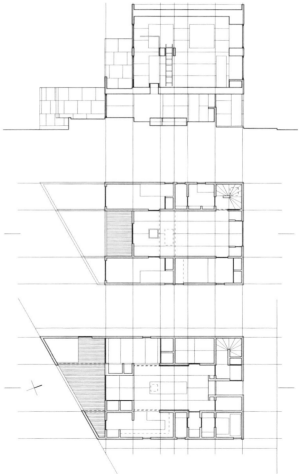

"Located in a dense area, the site is hemmed in by neighboring homes, a narrow street in front, and train tracks that cut across diagonally at the rear."

House with Studio for a Flower Artist; Hiroshi Nakao with Hiroko Serizawa; Saitama Prefecture

Opposite: This home and studio for a photographer consists of an outer shell of wood cladding supported by eleven massive ribs of engineered wood, and a *tatami*-floored inner core containing all the essentials for one.

Overleaf: Located in the foothills of the Japanese Alps, the house's blocky form stands out against a backdrop of snow-covered peaks and dense forest.

The Kobe earthquake January 1995 left a deep impression on the owner of this house. A freelance photographer from Tokyo, he happened to be in Kansai at the time of the tragedy. After witnessing firsthand how the lifeline of the local population was severed in an instant, he resolved to move his home to a place where he could be more self-sufficient. Since photo shoots require frequent trips to remote locations, he was not tied to the city, and as a single man he had no family obligations. He gave up access to Tokyo's restaurants and convenience stores and moved to the country.

The land he purchased, located in Yamanashi Prefecture two hours from Tokyo, sits at the base of the snow-capped Japanese Alps, where terraced fields, rice paddies, and greenery of every shade imaginable fan out below. The gently sloping property made it easy for architects Manami Takahashi and Chiharu Sugi to decide how to position the house. The dramatic site, however, required a bold response. Their solution is a simple building blending traditional sensibilities with the strength of engineered wood; it was completed in 1999.

Though the client requested a clean volume and minimal living spaces, the "house-within-a-house" organizational concept came from the architects. Concealed by the house's flat-roofed, rectangular outer shell is a second box containing a single multipurpose room that functions as the kitchen, bedroom, sitting room, and darkroom. It can even accommodate overnight guests who are brave enough to sleep on its tile-covered, rail-less top. With mats for sitting and movable panels for enclosure, this cozy, human-scaled room has almost everything the client needs.

Built-in appliances and cabinetry enclose the room on two sides like a thick wall, and the wooden floor in the middle of the room acts as a traditional-style staging area for the room's ever-changing functions. Here, a low table, cushions, and bedding can be taken out or stowed away as needed. On the room's other two sides, plastic *shoji*-inspired sliding doors can be pushed back to convert the room from an intimate nest for one to an airy platform open to the surrounding shell. The tiny room's heated floor is the house's most comfortable spot in winter; in summer, its decklike extension is the ideal place to catch a cool breeze or enjoy a cookout at its built-in *irori* hearth.

Nearly twice as big as the diminutive inner box in both plan and section, the oblong, concrete-floored shell is a cavernous, double-height enclosure whose semipermeable skin modulates the influx of daylight but not the sound of plows, the smell of freshly cut grass, or the feel of winter's frigid air. The shell resembles the traditional farmhouse's *doma*, a dirt-floored area where tools were stored, meals prepared, and, sometimes, animals housed. Like the *doma*, the shell is a transitional space between inside and out.

At the west end of the house is a third component that contains the garage downstairs and the photographer's studio above. A glass partition visually connects the second floor workroom to the rest of the house and admits views of the landscape at the other end.

The bathroom is contained in a concrete box jutting out from the house's south side. A bright oasis, the white-tiled bathroom is washed in daylight from an operable skylight directly above the tub. A strip window low to the floor is perfectly positioned to frame an oblique view of Mount Fuji, enabling the bather to enjoy the scenery without compromising privacy.

Made of wood, the house's exterior walls consist of fixed panels on top and movable parts at the base: louver-covered windows that moderate sunlight and air, or oversized wood *tobira* sliding glass panels that take advantage of the view. At the east end of the house, where the land slopes gently down, huge hinged glass doors open accordian style, and the concrete floor extends out as the terrace. By pushing and pulling, the client can turn his barnlike interior into a semioutdoor space.

As in many historical houses, enclosure and structure are completely independent. Eleven sturdy ribs, each one 18.37 feet high by 20 feet wide (5.6 meters high by 6 meters wide), buttress the house. Beautifully textured, the brawny wood elements are reminiscent of the magnificent, handmade beams and columns that support traditional *minka* houses. Unlike their antecedents — tree trunks with their bark planed off — these structural elements are made of engineered wood from the United States. They rely not on pin connections to hold their vertical and horizontal pieces together but, rather, on an integrated system ten times stronger than Japan's standard wood frame construction. Though massive, the man-made structural ribs help bridge the gap between the landscape's monumentality and the scale of human habitation.

"The land...located in Yamanashi Prefecture two hours from Tokyo, sits at the base of the snow-capped Japanese Alps, where terraced fields, rice paddies, and greenery of every shade imaginable fan out below."

House in the Woods; Chiharu Sugi + Manami Takahashi / Plannet Works; Yamanashi Prefecture

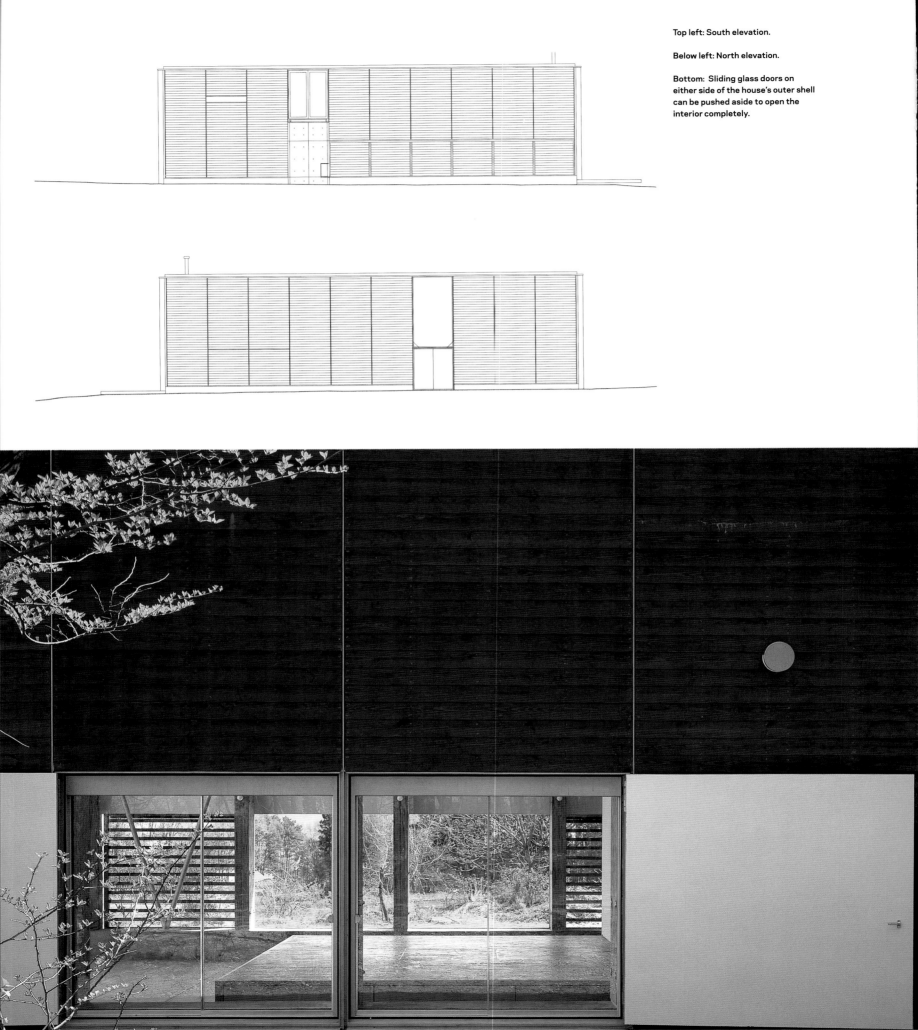

Top left: South elevation.

Below left: North elevation.

Bottom: Sliding glass doors on either side of the house's outer shell can be pushed aside to open the interior completely.

Above left: Contained within a discrete box attached to the house, the bathroom enjoys a spectacular view.

Above right: Straddling the stylistic line between East and West, the house has both a traditional Japanese *irori* hearth embedded in its *tatami* floor and a freestanding fireplace stationed at one end.

Right: Ground-floor plan (top); second-floor plan (bottom).

Overleaf: A pleasing composition of squares and proportional rectangles, the house is both dramatic in scale and a cozy retreat.

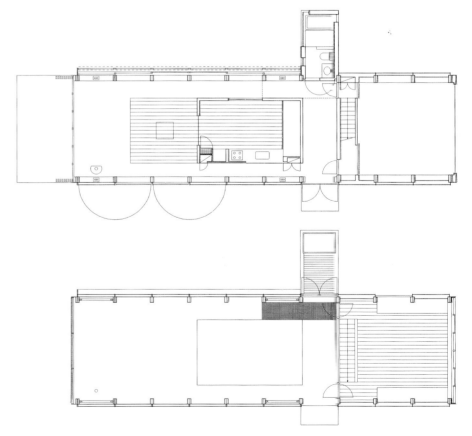

"Made of wood, the house's exterior walls consist of fixed panels on top and movable parts at the base: louver-covered windows that moderate sunlight and air, or oversized wood *tobira* sliding glass panels to take advantage of the view."

House in the Woods; Chiharu Sugi + Manami Takahashi / Plannet Works; Yamanashi Prefecture

The recent spate of vacation homes in Japan indicates that relaxation may be catching on. The demand for contemporary *besso*, or second homes, has steadily increased since they appeared on the market in the 1960s. For clients the country retreat can be a much-needed antidote to daily life. For architects it is an opportunity to test artistic concepts free from immutable, and often undesirable, external circumstances.

Although Japan's extreme urban conditions bring out the creative best in some, most architects would leap at an opportunity to build where restrictions are minimal and land is relatively bountiful.

"It is easy to experiment with weekend houses," says architect Shigeru Ban, who launched his career building paper-tube houses in the woods. Because weekend houses are used only sporadically or for short periods, they generally come with fewer programmatic requirements. Once temperatures drop and warm weather comes to an end, many houses go into hibernation altogether, eliminating the need for auxiliary heating systems and other winterization. As in the West, the owners of most vacation homes are happy to leave formality in the city, preferring casual rooms and free-flowing space. Though practical concerns often take precedence in town, second-home clients are frequently eager for something new. "Clients want and expect a quite different experience in a weekend house," explains Ban. Separating the bath from the rest of the house may be unusual and inconvenient in the city, but in the country this type of reshuffling can be novel and refreshing.

Beyond city limits, architects are also released from the stringent external conditions they face in town. Country sites are not free of legal limitations — almost no property in Japan is entirely immune to setbacks, site density, and height restrictions — but the torturous conditions architects contend with in urban areas are conspicuously absent. Compared with their counterparts in America or Europe, country properties in Japan are generally smaller and less isolated. Yet unlike infill sites in Tokyo or Osaka, they are still large enough for object-like houses with irregular geometries.

Still, some exurban sites come with their own peculiar requirements. Just ninety minutes from Tokyo, Kamakura is a popular seaside retreat and a historic mecca all in one. Because of its significance as Japan's capital during the Kamakura *bakufu,* or shogunate, government (1192–1336), local officials do not take new construction lightly, and many properties must be scoured for archaeological relics before construction can even commence. And the town of Shimoda, a beach area three hours from Tokyo, required Tokyo architects Astrid Klein and Mark Dytham to cap their new house with a pitched roof, since the site is near a national park.

The appeal of the vacation house lies in its contrasts and complements to city life. As anywhere else, the separation from worldly possessions and daily routines can be very liberating. Living with nature does wonders for restoring the spirit and revive the body. In Japan, where most city dwellers call tiny houses and apartments home, additional space alone is a remarkable luxury. "Some people have places both in and outside the city," explains architect Yoko Kinoshita. "A divided lifestyle raises the overall standard of living." Japan's Government Housing Loan Corporation couldn't agree more. With an eye to improving the quality of life, they launched the Pastoral House Loans campaign in 1998, whose express purpose was to stimulate the construction of second homes outside of major metropolitan areas.

Even with government help, not everyone can afford to maintain and live in more than one place. Though second homes are not new to Japan — the ruling classes have always enjoyed multiple residences — country houses for the general population are a fairly recent phenomenon that correlates with Japan's expanding wealth. Immediately after World War II, few could afford a primary residence, let alone a secondary one. As Japan's affluence blossomed, the construction and acquisition of country homes followed.

A country retreat requires not only surplus cash but also spare time, and people in Japan are reluctant to take time off. "Japanese people are not used to country houses," says architect Atsushi Yagi. "They are not very good at just taking it easy." Though Japan's calendar year is filled with national holidays, most people take one week of vacation per year, two weeks at the most. While some visit their second homes year round or over the New Year holiday, many people confine their usage to the warm summer months. "It's difficult for Japanese just to sit still on vacation," says architect Motomu Uno. "They prefer shorter vacation time with lots of activity." As a result, many country homes function as staging areas for mountain hikes, golf outings, and barbecue parties.

An island nation with a spine of mountains down the middle, Japan has its share of picturesque scenery. While there is no shortage of places to build second homes, there is a tendency to go where others have gone before. Unlike in the United States, where practically any land beyond the city limits is acceptable, very few people in Japan would consider farmland, for example, a suitable destination. Even beach homes have been slow to catch on. Not only is the water generally too cold for swimming, but towns and villages are already populated with fulltime residents who depend on the sea for their livelihood.

Yet second-home communities do exist near the ocean. Those outside Tokyo, Odawara, Oiso, Hayama, and Zushi, for example, host a mixture of full- and part-time residents. Others prefer the mountains. "Tokyo is very uncomfortable in the summer," says architect Fumihiko Maki. "Plateaus in the mountains and the seashore are the best places to escape the heat."

This was certainly one of the reasons missionaries began building country homes in Karuizawa during the Meiji period (1868–1912) at the end of the nineteenth century. Prior to 1885, when Alexander Croft Shaw, archdeacon of the Church of England, visited Karuizawa for the first time, the town was just another post-station stop in Nagano Prefecture. The area's natural wooded beauty, which reminded Shaw of his hometown in Scotland, inspired the construction of his country villa there in 1888. Soon after, other missionaries, business people, diplomats, and upper-class Japanese with a taste for Western-style architecture followed suit. As their chalet-style cottages and charming wood bungalows filled in the town's grid of tree-lined lanes, Karuizawa was transformed into one of Japan's first *bessochi*, or second-home communities.

Among the foreigners who became enchanted with Karuizawa was the Czech-American architect Antonin Raymond and his wife Noemi, a designer in her own right. Though the Raymonds initially came to Japan to work on Frank Lloyd Wright's Imperial Hotel, in due course they parted ways with Wright and set up their own office. The Raymonds completed many commercial projects as well as houses, especially after the 1923 earthquake, when they received numerous commissions for first and second homes from foreigners and Japanese alike.

The house garnering the most attention was their very own Karuizawa villa, completed in 1933. Built by local carpenters out of native stone, timber from nearby mountains, and readily available thatch, the house was a pastiche of indigenous materials assembled in a new way. "It has a very strong Japanese flavour, although it does not adopt any traditional Japanese forms," wrote Antonin Raymond in his autobiography. Like many traditional Japanese houses, this villa was topped by a pitched roof, but instead of pointing up in the middle, it pointed down. Tied together with an internal ramp, the house was inspired by an unrealized project designed by Le Corbusier for a site in South America, according to Raymond.

Some thirty years later, Karuizawa again witnessed a milestone in the history of Japan's second-home design. Following in the footsteps of his mentor, Raymond protégé Junzo Yoshimura completed a Karuizawa villa of his own in 1962. In contrast to Raymond's made-to-order houses for the elite, Yoshimura's modest residence paved the way for a whole new class of weekend retreats geared toward ordinary Japanese. Though Yoshimura designed the house for himself, it became a prototype that influenced the development of second homes in Japan as a whole.

The notion that one needn't be a millionaire to own a weekend retreat was just one of the novelties embodied in Yoshimura's house. The project also addressed practical concerns particular to vacation houses, such as balancing openness with the need for security when the house was unoccupied. Habitable spaces are contained within a square wooden box perched on a concrete pedestal. A glorified stair tower, the masonry base provides the only access up to the combined living and dining room, bedrooms, bathrooms, and kitchen. Above that are a tiny *tatami* room and study for one connecting to a private porch. Combining the best of both worlds, the main room is oriented toward an impressive stone fireplace that would be at home in any English country cottage, but is wrapped on two sides with traditional *amado* sliding panels.

By ushering in a new era for second homes, Yoshimura's house ultimately heralded change for the town of Karuizawa. Today many of the Western-style houses have been replaced with more contemporary Japanese homes. In order to ferry spectators to and from the 1998 Nagano Olympics, the bullet train was routed through town, putting Karuizawa within commuting distance of Tokyo. Yet even as large resort hotels and shopping malls sprang up near the station, the town's residential area has retained its exclusivity. "For Japanese, Karuizawa has a special meaning: It is old and established like New York's Hamptons and parts of New England," says Uno.

One hundred years after Karuizawa's birth as a *bessochi*, Japan witnessed another vacation-house building boom, stimulated by the Bubble period economy. More suburban settlement than quaint country town, the new *bessochi* consisted of small sites and bland houses. Catering to the surfeit of disposable income, developers bought up, subdivided, and sold off land together with prefabricated houses as package deals. "Japanese clients tend to go for the 'morning set,' eggs, toast, and coffee," explains architect Hitoshi Abe. Yet some property owners prefer to hire architects of their own choosing.

For architects accustomed to dealing with extreme urban conditions, a *bessochi* property can be a chance to try something new. Out in the country, architects have the freedom to focus on the house itself and its relationship to the natural landscape. For many, pure aesthetics and platonic forms are the starting points of the design process. Instead of neighboring houses and street fronts, they take their cues from view, topography, and foliage, determining the relationship between those natural features and the interior space.

Elevation of Junzo Yoshimura's country retreat in Karuizawa.

Antonin Raymond's Karuizawa villa.

Perhaps the two most distinctive characteristics that differentiate country and city houses are the way they make the transition from inside to out and their degree of openness. Vacation homes run the gamut from completely permeable to completely closed. Whether for reasons of security or privacy, some clients simply prefer sheltered and inward-facing homes, even out in the country. At the other end of the spectrum are those houses that incorporate traditional motifs such as *engawa* porches and sliding doors that can be pushed aside to let light and air mingle freely.

As in the United States, many country homes appear as pristine objects in the forest; however, the Japanese *besso* is not quite congruent with the American country cottage. More so than in the West, the Japanese vacation home is an antidote to city life. For the architect, it can be a chance to explore a different design process generated by abstract, aesthetic ideas rather than concrete, confining circumstances. In the country, architects can make buildings any shape they want. In Japanese cities, architects rarely have that option.

"By painting the house and its components white, Kuma intended to draw attention to nature's palette."

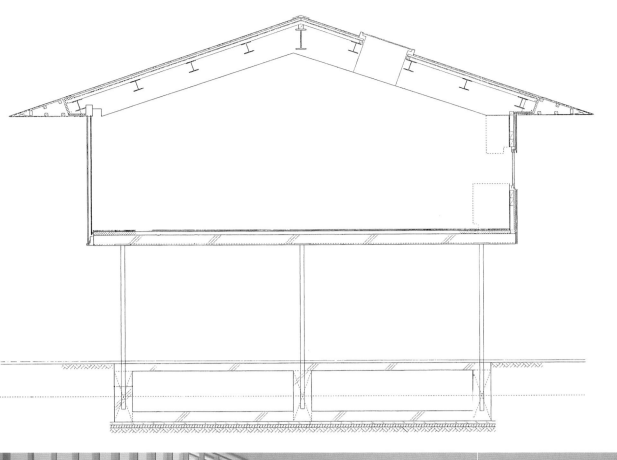

Previous pages: Elevated above the ground, Forest / Floor combines a traditional Japanese tearoom and sleek Western-style living areas under one massive white roof.

Left: Cross section.

Below: Sliding screens of slender metal slats shield the outdoor entry foyer without compromising the view. The glass front door (right) leads into the living area.

This country home, designed by Kengo Kuma for a department-store executive and his wife, unites a contemporary, Western-style living area and a traditional Japanese tearoom in a single volume. Though capped by one massive, pitched roof, the East and West architectures barely meet at floor level. Their only direct connection is a 24-inch (60-centimeter) square *nijiriguchi* doorway, an opening so low to the floor that guests must crawl to get from one side to the other. While the modern quarters are abstract and white, the traditional room is dark and composed of textured, natural materials. And while the combined living and dining room and kitchen is functionally flexible, the tearoom prescribes who sits where and what they will see.

In the past, many tearooms occupied their own freestanding huts — providing the owner had land. Surrounded by greenery and separated from the main house, these tiny buildings were spiritual havens removed from daily life. By contrast, Forest/Floor's version is almost completely absorbed within the house, and the site, though large, is not secluded. Located in the heart of an established vacation-home community and completed in 2003, Kuma's house shares a large property with two wood dwellings, one the client's former weekend retreat (now used by his daughter) and the other belonging to his mother.

Like the existing buildings, Forest/Floor is elevated 8.5 feet (2.6 meters) off the ground; its glass facade looks out at soaring pine trees, leafy Japanese maples, and a blanket of moss. "The best place to experience the forest is not at ground level but from the second floor," explains Kuma. Held up by two substantial columns, one concealed in shadow and the other inside a storage room, Kuma's white house appears to float. It has no solid base, and its ground floor is almost completely open.

Raising the house not only capitalizes on the view, it also allows cool air to blow humidity out from under the house and provides a sheltered parking area. A run of wafer-thin steel steps connects the carport to the screen-enclosed porch one flight up. The screen's sliding panels are reminiscent of the exterior-mounted louvers that shielded windows on traditional houses. Though similarly proportioned, Kuma's slender slats are made of white-painted steel, not wood. By painting the house and its components white, Kuma intended to draw attention to nature's palette. "The house should be a simple frame to see those colors and not have any color itself," says the architect. The porch, a quasi-outdoor room where East and West overlap, is both an extension of the tearoom and the entry foyer to the living room.

The house is symmetrical in plan and consists of a combined living/dining room and kitchen in the middle flanked by bedrooms and bathrooms on one side and the tearoom and its preparation area on the other. Created with the help of an expert carpenter, the tearoom counts many traditional features: *tatami* floors to sit on, a *tokonoma* alcove for a seasonal flower arrangement and a wall-mounted scroll, and *tsuchikabe* walls made of rammed earth. Enclosed by sliding *shoji* paper screens, the room showcases not just selected items from the client's extensive collection of tea paraphernalia but his skill as a tea master. When the movable panels are pushed open, the natural landscape outside becomes a visible part of the tearoom — a contemporary application of the borrowed scenery concept. "After eating a Western-style dinner in the Western dining room, it is an ideal place to sip brandy and experience the darkness of the forest," explains the architect.

In addition to its quotations from traditional Japan, Forest/Floor bears a striking resemblance to Mies van der Rohe's Farnsworth House in Plano, Illinois of 1951. "My first idea was to make an elevated floor in the forest," explains Kuma. "Then I linked it to the Farnsworth House." Indeed, both are white, single-story buildings wrapped with glass and lifted off the ground. Yet conceptually they are almost opposites. "The goal of Western modernism was the minimal box," says Kuma. But Kuma tried to erase that box by covering his house with a traditional hipped roof whose 5-foot-deep (1.5-meter-deep) eaves mask the house's rectilinear shape with shadow.

While Mies van der Rohe left the Farnsworth House structural frame exposed on the outside of the building, Kuma buried his two 24-inch-diameter (60-centimeter-diameter) concrete columns behind walls and closets. They support steel bars shaped like two giant umbrellas that hold up the roof but are hidden within the cathedral ceiling. A secondary set of white painted steel columns stands on the ground level. The field of columns orders the open space with a light touch.

Recalling the natural and man-made patterns of materials and architectural components in the traditional wood house, Forest/Floor's column grid, window sashes, sliding screens, and staircase treads are all composed of groups of repetitive, orthogonal lines. Though each cluster of lines is oriented in a different direction and spaced at a different interval, the various patterns together create a rich visual collage.

Part of their beauty comes from the remarkable thinness of each individual piece. Using steel enabled Kuma to shave centimeters off door frames, window frames, and hand railings. Even the edges of the roof eaves, which are normally quite thick, were reduced to a 0.8-inch-thick (2-centimeter-thick) line. Inside, square-sectioned white metal piping supports the glass-topped coffee and dining tables Kuma designed especially for the house. Sleek and elegant, the tables are comfortably proportioned to the human body, yet have a strong architectural expression.

"Inside, square-sectioned white metal piping supports the glass-topped coffee and dining tables Kuma designed especially for the house."

Forest / Floor; Kengo Kuma & Associates; Nagano Prefecture

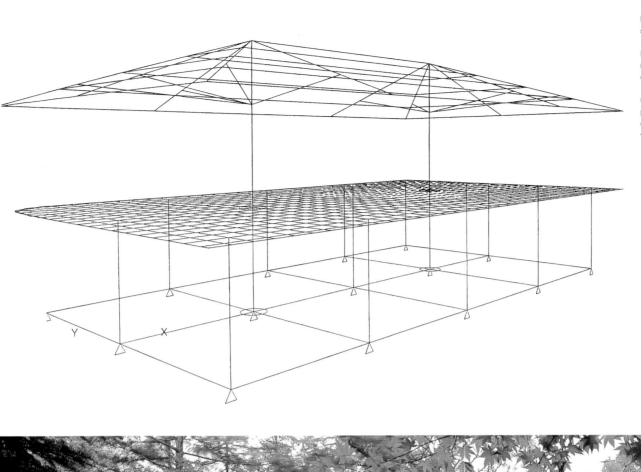

Left: Axonometric drawing of structural frame.

Below: At dusk, the illuminated rooms appear to hover over the delicate row of structural columns.

Opposite: Thin steel stair treads practically float as they connect the covered parking area below with the house above.

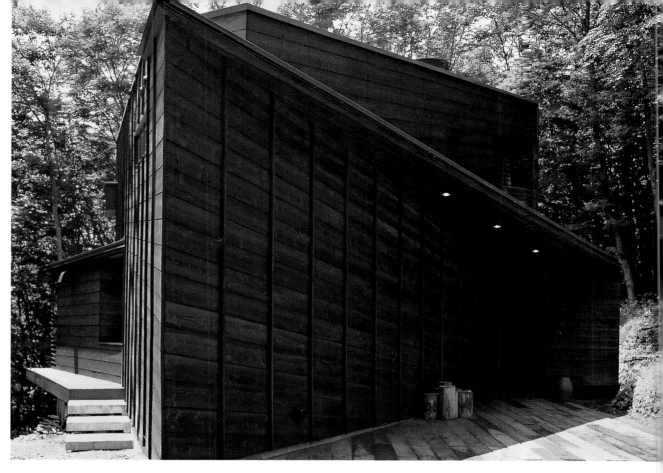

In designing the Yomiuri Media Miyagi Guesthouse, a weekend retreat completed in 1998 at the base of Zao Mountain, architect Hitoshi Abe took his inspiration from the hilly land. Aside from its topography, the property, located in a second-home development ninety minutes from the city of Sendai, came with relatively few restrictions. To determine where to put the building, Abe began by stretching a length of ribbon across a contoured site model. This simple gesture ended up defining the shape of the building. As he shifted the ribbon this way and that, Abe noticed that it molded itself to and took on the profile of the land. From there, transferring the shape of the simple strip of cloth to architectural fabric was easy.

A 1,850-square-foot (172-square-meter) wood box overlooking a densely forested ravine, the house is a marriage of the familiar and the utterly foreign. Traditional signs of domesticity, such as rectangular walls and pitched roofs, are missing, yet the building's irregular shape seems right at home in the forest. Its concise plan consists of living, dining, and kitchen areas as well as the bathroom downstairs, a *tatami* room and a bedroom upstairs. Its muted materials blend harmoniously with the powerful natural setting, but its dynamic spiraling form is startling.

The genesis of that form was the ribbon itself. The house's dark wood wall retraces the ribbon's path. It wraps the house perimeter and then loops around a second time to enclose a double-height, multipurpose room at the heart of the house. Oblique angles and sharp corners complete the ribbon's overall shape, and changing wall heights mirror its ups and downs. From the foremost corner of the house, the wall expands dramatically in two directions, sloping down to the front door but at the same time climbing steadily up toward the trees.

This divergence is underscored by the walls' outer surface, a pastiche of board-and-batten construction. Some sides are made of orthogonal wood planks or a conventional crosshatch of vertical strips and horizontal boards. Others consist of skewed grids that negotiate changes in height from one end of the wall to the other. Though the house's concrete base neutralizes the bumpy ground surface and anchors the house firmly, its slanting lines and tilting roof planes make it appear frozen in midrotation.

The front door is a massive wood slab with a delicate disguised handle that blends in with the outer skin. Windows pierce the wall, and where it wraps around the covered porch at the back of the house, Abe substituted horizontal louvers for fixed planks. Abe wanted to preserve the wall's integrity, so he was careful not to excise too much solid surface. With good reason, the clients wanted shelter from the outdoors — since snowfalls in this part of Japan tend to be heavy. "Usually when there is a beautiful landscape outside, you try to make the house as transparent as possible," explains Abe. "But this time they went for a more protected feel." In fact, a single picture window provides the only direct view out from the main room.

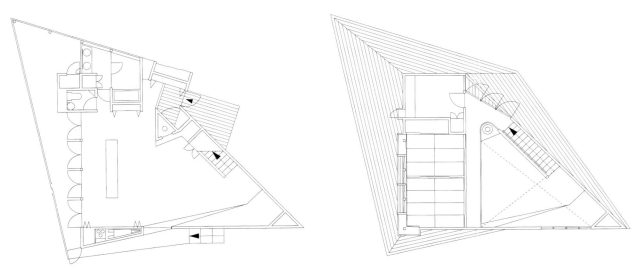

Opposite: The heart of the house is its double-height living room which flows into the dining room at the rear. Stairs lining the living room's angled wall connect to a second floor *tatami*-mat room sequestered behind *shoji* screens.

Far left: First-floor plan.

Left: Second-floor plan.

Below: The rear of the house is wrapped with an enclosed outdoor porch. The angled projecting volume contains a small, closet and the toilet enclosure, approached from the inside.

"Wood ceiling, walls, and floor are balanced by light accents such as the white plasterboard stair enclosure, shoji screens and shiny tiled surfaces that give the bathing area its clean and clinical look."

"In designing the Yomiuri Media Miyagi Guesthouse, a weekend retreat completed in 1998 at the base of Zao Mountain, architect Hitoshi Abe took his inspiration from the hilly land."

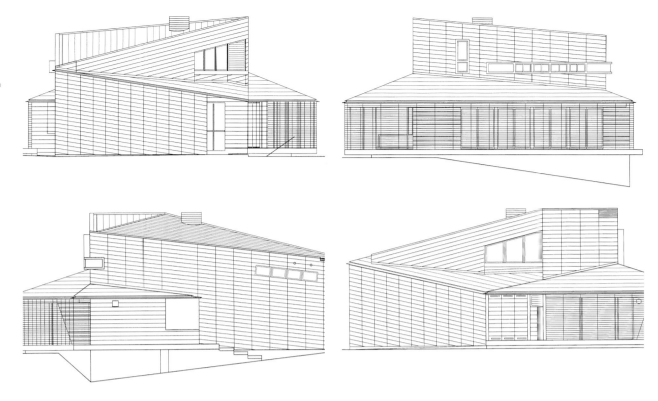

The house is used for various work-related events, such as seminars and presentations, so the clients wanted the interior to be as flexible as possible. An advertising executive, his wife and their grown daughter, the clients also come from Sendai to hike, garden and collect wild mushrooms.

In light of the houses dual purpose Abe decided that the best strategy was to make a huge open space surrounded by subsidiary rooms. The heart of the house is a double-height triangular room. One side is lined with built-in storage, another contains stairs to the second floor, and the third is open to the adjacent dining area. A homey fireplace in one corner completes the picture. The epitome of flexibility, the room is big enough for parties and performances and still cozy enough for intimate family gatherings.

Where the ceiling drops to single height the main room flows into the dining area. Running along the back of the house, it is flanked by a modest galley kitchen at one end and toilet and the bath at the other. In contrast to the main room, where the ceiling appears to float, the dining area's ceiling hovers protectively above the table for ten. Glass French doors open onto the wedge-shaped engawa overlooking the ravine. Crossed with shadows by day and illuminated by floodlights at night, the indoor-outdoor room is the ideal spot to survey the scenery.

Overhead on the second floor is a dormlike, fourteen-mat tatami room that can hold up to twenty sleeping bags — a necessity when accommodating visiting dance troupes and other large groups of overnight guests. Movable shoji screens separate it from a balcony overlooking the main space and sliding fusuma wall panels can divide the room in two when the family members are alone.

Throughout the house, upstairs, downstairs, inside and out, dark wood is ubiquitous. It both symbolizes Abe's ribbon and references the minka rural house where the client grew up. Yet Abe's rendition is much more light-hearted than the traditional, heavy-beamed house where most of the living space is constantly in shadow. Throughout the interior there is play between dark and light surfaces. Wood ceiling, walls, and floor are balanced by light accents such as the white plasterboard stair enclosure, shoji screens and shiny tiled surfaces that give the bathing area its clean and clinical look.

There are houses with screened porches; and then, as with House +, there are screened porches with houses. A weekend retreat designed by Tokyo architect Atsushi Yagi, this solitary, white, block like building consists of a mesh-wrapped enclosure shaped like a basketball court plus a narrow wood box containing the standard functional elements of combined kitchen and living/dining rooms on the first floor and two bedrooms on the second. Though the two exist side by side on a concrete base, they are far from equal. The interior rooms are small, dark, and compact, while the porch is a glorious, light-filled space that straddles the line between inside and out.

A house with this amount of exposure would be out of place in the city, but it is well suited to the country. Designed for two sisters in their sixties, the house, built in 1999, is located in a planned second-home community at the base of Mount Fuji, about an hour from Tokyo by car. The older sister, a freelance editor who wanted a place to work far away from her usual Tokyo haunts, bought the property; the younger sister paid the construction bills. Together they dreamed of building a weekend house they could enjoy both with their individual families and as a group.

Apart from these general goals and the number and size of rooms, the clients had very few requests. Neither did Yagi get much guidance from the 5,382-square-foot (500-square-meter) site. It came with some restrictions regarding density and setbacks that were determined by the community, but the most limiting factor was the property's steep slope, that precluded a large yard or garden. The architect set out to invent a new type of indoor-outdoor space where his clients could enjoy the natural environment without compromising their comfort.

Instead of trying to move mountains, Yagi kept the land much as it was and built an artificial ground plane from concrete. Painted white to match the silvery mesh, the platform levels the ground and lifts the building. It also mediates between the man-made and natural environments. Tucked away in one corner and camouflaged by a metal gate, a staircase leads from parking to porch. The house may not have a dominant facade, but its grand entry court more than compensates

Forecourt is just one of the porch's many roles. A remarkably versatile two-story space, it is big enough to accommodate everything from barbecue parties to badminton matches. The grandchildren can even play catch without having to chase after errant balls lost in the woods. "You can't do that on an ordinary wood deck," chuckles Yagi. Lit by surface-mounted lamps, the porch remains a fully functioning outdoor room long after the sun has set.

The screened enclosure glows like a giant *andon* lantern at night; during the day, it shimmers in the sunlight. Composed of two layers of mesh, one stainless steel and the other translucent plastic, the screens are held in place by slender steel columns that connect to the corrugated plastic roof 16 feet (5 meters) above. "The roof is so high you can't really tell where it is," says Yagi. Like a giant filter, the screens' overlapping square openings are big enough to let in abundant light and fresh air yet small enough to keep out all but the heaviest downpour. They eliminate the need for *katori senko*, a mosquito-repelling incense, a mainstay of most country homes.

A true blend of inside and out, the cagelike porch with its semipermeable skin is thoroughly embedded in the surrounding forest. At the same time, its shielding barrier and raised base ally it with the sheltered interior. Roof aligns with roof, and painted concrete floor connects effortlessly with its wood-covered counterpart. While Yagi would have happily eliminated the wall separating the two halves of the building, that would have cost too much. He settled for wood stained a quiet shade of brown, and he inserted glass wherever possible. Downstairs, sliding doors that unveil a 12-foot-wide (3.6-meter-wide) opening fuse the two parts. Upstairs, windows fill the sleeping quarters with muted daylight and fresh air. By orienting openings on both floors toward the porch, Yagi was able to limit his use of exterior glass. Even in a *bessochi*, privacy can be a real concern.

Within the house, the preservation of privacy and demarcation of individual space did not concern Yagi. Family members use the bedrooms interchangeably, one Western-style and the other *tatami* floored, by rolling out *futon* as needed. By keeping rooms uncluttered, Yagi was able to distinguish this house from its owners' full-time residences in the city. "One purpose of a weekend house is to separate from the usual lifestyle," he explains.

The only truly private place in the house is the bath. Inspired by traditional *onsen* hot spring spas whose communal baths are frequently located in their own separate pavilion. Yagi isolated the tub and changing area in a cozy room of their own on the far side of the porch. Though this degree of separation from the living areas might cause some consternation on a daily basis, it is a welcome weekend change from routine that rewards users with a quiet, contemplative spot to appreciate the scenery while soaking in the warm water.

"A true blend of inside and out, the cagelike porch with its semipermeable skin is thoroughly embedded in the surrounding forest."

House +; Atsushi Yagi Architects & Associates; Shizuoka Prefecture

Opposite: Composed of two screened layers, one stainless steel and the other plastic, the court's covering is supported by steel columns that also hold up its corrugated-plastic roof.

Right: When the sliding glass doors are pushed back, the covered court becomes an extension of the first-floor living/dining room and kitchen beyond.

Below: The combined living/dining room is awash in daylight from the adjacent court.

Below: West elevation (top); section (bottom).

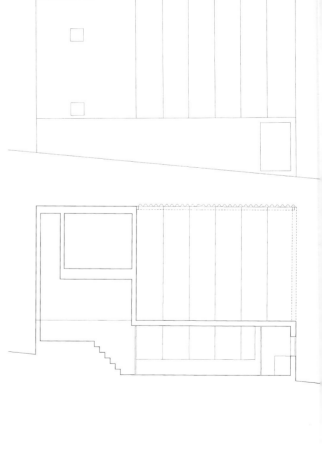

"Located in the wilds of Gunma Prefecture, the 1,400-square-foot (130-square-meter) home was completed in 1998."

Weekend House; Office of Ryue Nishizawa; Gunma Prefecture

Previous pages: Weekend House's black metal wrapping completely disguises its light, airy, one-room interior loosely divided by glass partitions and courtyard gardens.

Opposite: A movable perimeter wall can be pushed aside to connect this courtyard garden to the surrounding interior environment.

Right: The interior space has an open plan accentuated by slender support columns.

Overleaf: While many country houses are designed to be as open as possible, Weekend House features only three small windows on the south side.

A fortresslike square box encased in corrugated black metal, Weekend House reveals nothing of its inner workings. Concealed within this tough shell is a light-filled oasis punctuated by internal courtyards and slender columns that divide the one-room home into lobby, kitchen, living, *tatami*, and sleeping areas. Solid walls sharply define the house on the outside; inside, glass sheets and filmy curtains do the same.

Located in the wilds of Gunma Prefecture, the 1,400-square-foot (130-square-meter) home was completed in 1998. Designed by Tokyo architect Ryue Nishizawa, it belongs to a housewife with a tiny apartment in Tokyo. To improve her quality of life she decided to build a second home that could double as a private gallery where her artist daughter could show her paintings. Although the property had been in the client's family for years, construction of the nearby highway interchange and the requisite clearing of the land provided the incentive to build. Despite the property's dramatic setting, surrounded by distant snowcapped mountains, the client wanted to keep windows to a minimum. Since neighbors are few and far between, security concerned her. She also wanted to fend off any intrusive curiosity seekers and block the sound of traffic from the convenient but noisy expressway.

The contradiction in creating a country house closed to the environment led Nishizawa to barricade the building but use courtyards to connect inside and out. Like *tsuboniwa*, tiny gardens that bring light and fresh air into the middle of traditional houses, Nishizawa's three courtyards are covered with daylight-admitting wood louvers. One court doubles as an entry foyer, and the other two are planted with small trees and shrubs that benefit from the client's gardening skills. Like their historical precedents, Nishizawa's gardens are visual focal points within the house, but the similarity between new and old stops there. Traditional courtyards sit in the middle of a house, while Nishizawa's are at the edge and open to the surrounding landscape at one end. In each one, fixed glass encases three sides, and movable panes the fourth. When pushed aside, the sliding walls reveal oblique views of the outdoors. When closed, they merge with the outer walls to seal the box from intruders.

Nishizawa initially proposed cladding the house exterior with plain wood, but even this was too conspicuous for the client. So he took the drastic step of swaddling the whole house with matte black metal sheets. This outer wrapping is quiet and understated, and helps the building recede into the landscape. Punctured by occasional windows, the anonymous black box is neither inviting nor easy to enter — simply finding the front door is a challenge.

Past this threshold, the home opens up like an exquisite jewel box. One courtyard, a 43-inch-wide (110-centimeter-wide) gravel-covered conduit, leads the way in. Transparent walls on either side of the narrow slot reveal the contents of the house all at once. A sliding door opens onto the lobby, a large room whose flat wall surfaces are perfect for hanging art. The *tatami* room and the living area, containing a televi-

"A fortresslike, square box encased in corrugated black metal, Weekend House reveals nothing of its inner workings."

Opposite: The largest of the three courtyard gardens is opposite the lobby, where it separates the combined living/dining-kitchen area from one of the two semi-enclosed bedrooms.

Below left: Amid atmospheric gridded light, the courtyard showcases a panoramic view of the interior.

Below right: Site plan (top) and floor plan (bottom).

sion set, antique *tansu* chest, and wood burning stove, can be seen through the layers of glass and forest of columns. While the house's one and only picture window defines the living area, a floating white counter designates the adjacent kitchen. In the other direction, the entry court separates the two glassed-in bedrooms — one barely wider than the bed itself — from the rest of the house. Next to the sleeping quarters and hidden behind solid walls and closed doors — the only ones in the house — are the bath and toilet.

Though the blond wood floor and grid of delicate, rust-colored wood columns unify the interior, furniture and lighting divide it into distinct functional zones. The courtyards do a little of both: Their transparent walls are physical barriers that break up space and divert traffic but also forge visual links between separate areas. As light filters down from above, ever-changing shadows pass through their large panes and dance across the wood floor. While solid exterior walls protect the owner's privacy, the use of extensive glass on the interior requires averted gazes and full-height curtains to block views. Even the bathroom's pedestal sink may be sequestered behind a circular curtain for those who prefer to brush their teeth in private.

Using curtains instead of walls and walls instead of windows is indeed a radical approach. Yet Weekend House is not completely divorced from tradition. Historical models may have inspired the courtyards, but the *tatami* area is an obvious tie to the past. The room also incorporates bits and pieces borrowed from the family's *minka* rural house that once stood on the property. Movable panels, albeit pivoting, not sliding, can shut off the room at one end, and a *tansu* taken from the old house occupies the seat of honor at the other. Though the chest was worn out, Nishizawa refurbished its doors and mounted the piece so that it appears to hover above the ground. The architect also borrowed the *daikokubashira*, the thick column that was the symbolic center of the old house. A main component of the *minka*'s structural frame, it is literally a shell of its former self. The old pillar standing prominently in the middle of the room was hollowed out to form a cover encasing a new column.

Visitors to Weekend House may experience a chilly reception from the exterior, but this impression melts away once inside, where warm wood, soft daylight, and traditional accent pieces make it easy to feel immediately at home.

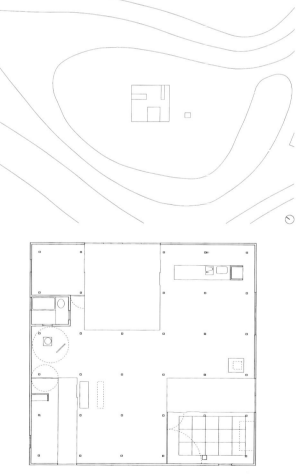

Villa Fujii
Motomu Uno + Phase Associates

Opposite: The owner's wing containing all the essential spaces (right) and the guest wing containing separate suites for two sets of grandparents (left) meet up at the entrance foyer (rear) but are also connected by a short stairway in between.

Below: Roof plan.

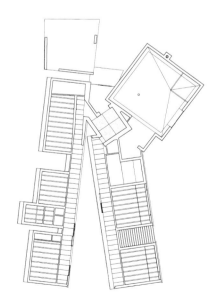

Karuizawa, the mountain retreat of choice for many in Japan's social register, was the birthplace of the modern country villa. Unlike its predecessors, the house Tokyo architect Motomu Uno built in 2000 treats nature as something to be seen only. Located in the heart of Karuizawa's historic residential district, Uno's Villa Fujii consists of two splayed wings that reach into the landscape like the best of traditional Japanese homes. But instead of movable panels and sliding screens, Uno used sheets of glass to seal the interior and frame the scenery like a photographic lens.

"The relationship between nature and artificial space has changed," says Uno. "For the older generation, it was about physical contact, but for the younger generation, it is a visual experience." This degree of separation might not appeal to everyone — having a country house is, after all, about being in the country. But Uno's client, who works for a giant American software company, was completely at home with virtual realities. In addition to the family's primary residence in a fashionable Tokyo neighborhood, the client wanted a home away from home where he could relax with his wife, their two school-age children, his parents, her parents — or completely by himself.

The client's job requires a great deal of overseas travel, thus transit time to and from his country villa was an important consideration. Just an hour from Tokyo Station by bullet train and practically surrounded by golf courses, Karuizawa was the ideal spot. The client purchased a 17,803-square-foot (1,654-square-meter) empty lot facing one of the town's charming, tree-lined lanes and commissioned Uno (an old school friend) for the project.

Uno began by assessing sight lines and geographic contours. This careful investigation convinced him that building the house toward the rear of the property would take best advantage of its wooded scenery and gentle slope. Given the land's size and exposure, Uno could have designed a pristine, objectlike building. Instead, Uno's top priority was to create a dialogue between the interior space and the landscape. "The composition of traditional villas like Kyoto's Katsura Rikyu [Katsura Detached Palace] is defined by the relationship between the interior space and landscape," he explains.

Putting a contemporary face on that age-old idea was Uno's intention in devising a two-pronged design with an uncovered exterior. The owners' wing, which includes all the essential rooms, can be used in tandem with or independent of the guest wing. The two sections are connected by a double-height, stone-floored entry hall bathed in muted daylight from the frosted skylight overhead. From there, steps lead to the guest wing, where a single-loaded corridor gives access to the client's study and sleeping quarters for each set of grandparents. Between the two bedrooms, one Western-style and the other *tatami* floored, is a Japanese-style bath

made of fragrant cedar wood but sized like an American luxury hot tub. Encased in glass and jutting out into the woods, the tub is equal parts nature conservatory and soaking pool.

On the other side, the entry hall connects to the owners' wing. One door leads to the master bedroom and bathrooms and the children's shared bunk room; another segues smoothly into the combined living/dining room. The consummate party space, it is a huge square room with a fireplace on one side and a pass-through kitchen on the other. Though comfortable and inviting, the expansive room is fitted with blond wood built-ins and sleek European furnishings that are elegant and timeless.

Hidden behind a woven bamboo screen, a doorway links the living room with the outdoor wood deck. The real connection with the environment is the room's dramatic L-shaped glass wall. The wall is composed of a horizontal 4-foot-tall (1.2-meter-tall) glass band wrapping around one corner of the room and abutting a huge vertical pane filling the entire 15-foot (4.6-meter) floor-to-ceiling height. While the tall window captures the soaring trees in all their leafy glory, the short one focuses on the mossy ground plane.

This low strip of glass with a blank wall above is at an ideal height for gazing outdoors while lounging on the sofa. It is reminiscent of the traditional teahouse's floor-level window, which framed views for *tatami*-seated patrons. "Even the position of furniture can have an important relationship with the outside," says Uno. Though blocking a potential view with a solid wall may seem counterintuitive in a house in the woods, it actually focuses the eye instead of letting it roam. It also showcases Uno's structural acumen. The hovering panels appearing to defy gravity are actually tied in place by steel tension rods overhead.

While some windows are for viewing others provide ventilation. Large fixed sheets of glass frame the scenery, and small operable windows, above or below eye level but not even with it, admit refreshing cross breezes. The glass panes of Uno's *enagwa* are anchored securely except where wood-slatted sliding doors take their place. These sliding doors open onto exterior steps that bridge the gap between the two wings and mediate the level change, creating a shortcut from one part of the house to the other.

Wedged between the two wings is an unusual triangular swath of open space dotted with randomly placed trees and overgrown with *kumazasa* ground cover. Despite its untamed appearance, the narrow space was only partly the work of nature. To further his goal of merging interior space and landscape, Uno teamed up with landscape architect Toru Mitani — an approach that is a throwback to Japan's premodern age, when carpenters and gardeners collaborated as a matter of course.

Mitani's overall strategy was to intervene as little as possible; he planted trees and trimmed grass only as

Opposite: An L-shaped window that directs the gaze either up to the trees or down to the ground plane encloses the dining area. Steel tension rods below the ceiling inside support a wall hovering over the low window.

Right: The dining room offers views of the landscape through a large expanse of fixed glass. A modest doorway concealed by a woven screen, at right, leads to an outdoor wood deck.

Below right: View from the guest wing past the narrow circulation spine to the owner's wing beyond.

Overleaf: A wood deck along one side of the house unites the owner's wing (left) and the public spaces (right). The deck connects to a raised wood walkway running through the garden.

needed. He followed the gentle slope of the land with a wooden walkway connecting the private deck to the public road located 4 feet (1.2 meters) below the site. Mitani's walk is reminiscent of the paths winding through many traditional Japanese gardens: it has a clear start and finish but creates switchbacks that offer a chance to pause, reflect, and survey the scene. As in many historical gardens, each alteration makes the landscape look even more natural than before.

"The real connection with the environment is the room's dramatic L-shaped glass wall."

Further Reading

General

Barrenche, Raul. *Modern House Three*. (London: Phaidon Press, 2005)

Carver, Norman F. Jr.. *Form and Space of Japanese Architecture*. (Tokyo: Shokokusha Publishing Co., 1955)

Coaldrake, William Howard. *The Way of the Carpenter*: Tools and Japanese Architecture. (New York: Weatherhill, Inc., 1991)

Daguerre, Mercedes. *20 Houses by 20 Architects*. (Milan: Electa Architecture, 2005)

Drexler, Arthur. *The Architecture of Japan*. (New York: The Museum of Modern Art, 1955)

Engel, Heinrich. *The Japanese House/ A Tradition for Contemporary Architecture*. (Tokyo: Charles E. Tuttle Company, 1964)

Fawcett, Chris. *The New Japanese House*. (London: Granada Publishing Limited, 1980)

Hibi, Sadao. *Japanese Detail: Architecture*. (San Francisco: Chronicle Books, 2002)

Jeremy, Michael & M.E. Robinson. *Ceremony and Symbolism in the Japanese Home*. (Manchester, England: Manchester University Press, 1989)

Jinnai, Hidenobu. Tokyo: *A Spatial Anthropology*. (Berkeley and Los Angeles, California: University of California Press, 1995)

Kawashima, Chuji. Minka: *Traditional Houses of Rural Japan*. (Tokyo: Kodansha International Ltd., 1986)

Keene, Marc P. *Japanese Garden Design*. (Tokyo: Charles E. Tuttle Company, 1996)

Melhuish, Clare. *Modern House 2*. (London: Phaidon Press, 2000)

Morse, Edward S. *Japanese Homes and their Surroundings*. (Tokyo: Charles E. Tuttle Company, Inc., 1972)

Phaidon Press (ed). *10 x 10*. (London: Phaidon Press, 2000)

Phaidon Press (ed). *10 x 10_2*. (London: Phaidon Press, 2005)

Phaidon Press (ed). *The Phaidon Atlas of Contemporary World Architecture*. (London: Phaidon Press, 2004)

Phaidon Press (ed). *The Phaidon Atlas of Contemporary World Architecture Travel Edition*. (London: Phaidon Press, 2005)

Stewart, David B.. *The Making of a Modern Japanese Architecture*. (Tokyo: Kodansha International Ltd., 1987)

Tanizaki, Jun'ichiro. *In Praise of Shadows*. (Tokyo: Charles E. Tuttle Company, Inc., 1984)

Tsuzuki, Kyoichi. *Tokyo Style*. (Kyoto: Kyoto Shoin Co., Ltd, 1993)

Ueda, Atsushi. *The Inner Harmony of the Japanese House*. (Tokyo: Kodansha International Ltd., 1990)

Welsh, John. *Modern House*. (London: Phaidon Press, 1995)

Zukowsky, John (editor). Japan 2000: *Architecture and Design for the Japanese Public*. (Munich: Prestel-Verlag, 1998)

Architect Monographs

Abe, Hitoshi. *Flicker*. (Tokyo: TOTO Shuppan, 2005)

Aoki, Jun. *Complete Works 1991-2004*. (Tokyo: INAX Shuppan, 2004)

Bognar, Botand. *Kengo Kuma: Selected Works*. (New York: Princeton Architectural Press, 2005)

Dal Co, Francesco. *Tadao Ando*. (London: Phaidon Press, 1995)

Endo, Shuhei. *Paramodern*. (Osaka: amus arts press, 2002)

Kitayama, Koh. *On the Situation*. (Tokyo: TOTO Shuppan, 2002)

Kuma, Kengo. *Kengo Kuma/ Materials, Structures, Details*. (Basel: Birkhauser-Publishers for Architecture, 2004)

McQuaid, Matilda. *Shigeru Ban*. (London: Phaidon Press, 2003)

Pare, Richard. *Tadao Ando: The Colours of Light*. (London: Phaidon Press, 1996)

Pare, Richard. *Tadao Ando: The Colours of Light*. (mini) (London: Phaidon Press, 2000)

Raymond, Antonin. *An Autobiography*. (Tokyo: Charles E. Tuttle Company, 1973)

Sejima, Kazuyo and Nishizawa, Ryue. *Kazuyo Sejima + Ryue Nishizawa/SANAA: Works 1995 - 2003*. (Tokyo: TOTO Shuppan, 2003)

Suzuki, Hiroyuki (ed). *Shuhei Endo*. (Milan: Electa Architecture, 2003)

Watanabe, Hiroshi. *Waro Kishi*. (Berlin: Edition Axel Menges, 2001)

House in a Plum Grove
Location: Tokyo
Year: 2004
Architect: Kazuyo Sejima & Associates
Principals: Yoshitaka Tanase, Junya Ishigami, Koji Yoshida
Consultants Sasaki Structural Consultants (structure),
System Design Laboratory (insulation)
General Contractor: Heisei Construction Company

c House
Location: Higasikurume-city, Tokyo
Year: 2000
Architect: Jun Aoki & Associates
Project Manager: Kumiko Inui
Structural Design: Kanebako Structural Engineers
General Contractor: Fukazawa Corporation

Natural Shelter
Location: Tokyo
Year: 1999
Architects: Masaki Endoh + Masahiro Ikeda / Endo Design House
+ mias / Masaki Endoh, Masahiro Ikeda, Kenji Nawa
General Contractor: Hou Onkyo Giken Co. Ltd.

UNS
Location: Tokyo
Year: 2001
Architect: Hiroyuki Arima + Urban Forth
Principal: Hiroyuki Arima
Project Manager: Toru Sakiyama
General Contractor: Miura Koumuten

T Set
Location: Setagaya-ku, Tokyo
Year: 2002
Architect: Chiba Manubu Architects
Structural Engineer: Structural Design Office OAK

Shutter House for a Photographer
Location: Minato-ku, Tokyo
Year: 2003
Architect: Shigeru Ban
Project Team: Shigeru Ban, Nobutaka Hiraga, Anne Scheou, Tomoo Nitta
Structural Engineer: Hoshino Engineers: Shuichi, Takashige Suzuki
Mechanical Engineer: S Associates

Ambi-Flux
Location: Shinbashi, Minato-ku, Tokyo
Year: 2001
Architect: Akira Yoneda / architecton
Structural Design: Masahiro Ikeda
Structural Engineer: Hisakatu Henmi / ES associates; Kazuhiro Endo / EOS
General Contractor: Taiyu Co.

Balcony House
Location: Tsuki-gun, Kanagawa Prefecture
Year: 2001
Architects: Takaharu + Yui / Tezuka Architects. Masahiro Ikeda / mias
Lighting Design: Masahide Kakudate / Masahide Kakudate Lighting
Architect & Associates

Introspective House
Location: Yamato-city, Kanagawa Prefecture
Year: 2001
Architect: Hiroyuki Arima + Urban Fourth
Principal: Hiroyuki Arima
Project Team: Seiichi Ishida, Nobuko Matsuo, Toru Sakiyama, Takeshi Hanamoto
Structural Engineer: Higuchi Associates
Mechanical Engineer: Ishikawa Setsubi Sekkei
General Contractor: Meito Kensetsu

S House
Location: Odawara-city, Kanagawa Prefecture
Year: 1996
Architect: Jun Aoki & Associates
Project Manager: Riko Tsuru
Structural Design: Kanebako Structural Engineers
General Contractor: Ogawa Construction Co., Ltd.

House in Higashi-Otsu
Location: Otsu-city, Shiga Prefecture
Year: 2003
Architect: Waro Kishi + K. Associates / Architects
Structural Engineer: Urban Design Institute
General Contractor: Kunisada Construction

Naked House
Location: Kawagoe-city, Saitama Prefecture
Year: 2000
Architect: Shigeru Ban Architects
Project Team: Shigeru Ban, Mamiko Ishida, Anne Scheou
Structural Engineers: Hoshino Architect & Engineer: Shuichi, Takashige Suzuki
General Contractor: Misawaya Kensetsu

tn House
Location: Meguro-ku, Tokyo
Year: 2000
Architect: ADH Architects
Structural Engineer: Umezawa Structural Engineers
Mechanical Engineer: Kankyo Engineering
General Contractor: Matsumoto Corporation

Chikada House
Location: Toshima-ku, Tokyo
Year: 1994
Architect: Makoto Motokura / Kenchiku Design Studio
Structural Engineer: TIS & Partners

Zig/Zag
Location: Setagaya-ku, Tokyo, Japan
Year: 2001
Architect: Nobuaki Furuya / Studio NASCA
Structural Engineer: Oak Structural Design Office
Mechanical Engineer: Tetens Engineering
General Contractor: Shinkou Corporation

House for a Vegetable Seller
Location: Shinbashi, Minato-ku, Tokyo
Year: 2001
Architects: Yoko Inoue / Atelier Knot
General Contractor: Module Giken
Structural Engineer: Hoshino Architects & Engineers

Healtecture K
Location: Takatsuki-city, Osaka Prefecture
Year: 1996
Architect: Shuhei Endo Architect Institute
Project Manager: Aoi Fujioka
Structural Engineer: SOUGO-JUTAKU
General Contractor: Shinichi Kiyosada

Plane + House
Location: Setagaya-ku, Tokyo
Year: 1999
Architect: Koh Kitayama + architectureWORKSHOP
Structural Engineer: Plus One Structural Des. & Eng. Firm
Mechanical Engineer: GOH Technical Design Studio
General Contractor: Daido-Kogyo

House with Studio for a Flower Artist
Location: Tokorozawa-city, Saitama Prefecture
Year: 1996
Architect: Hiroshi Nakao with Hiroko Serizawa
General Contractor: Manzzo Koumusho

House in the Woods
Location: Yamanashi Prefecture
Year: 1999
Architect: Chiharu Sugi + Manami Takahashi / Plannet Works
Principals: Chiharu Sugi + Manami Takahashi, Kenji Ikemoto, Masayohi Otsubo
Structural Engineer: TIS & Partners.
Mechanical Engineer: San Mechanical Engineers
General Contractor: Nitsu-Gumi Co. Ltd.

Forest / Floor
Location: Nagano Prefecture
Year: 2003
Building Area: 453.67 ft2 / 138.28 m2
Architect: Kengo Kuma & Associates; Toshio Yada
Structural Engineers: Makino Structural Design; Satomi Makino, Ikuko Okamoto
Mechanical Engineers: P.T. Morimura & Associates LTD.

Yomiuri Media Miyagi Guesthouse
Location: Katta-gun, Miyagi Prefecture
Year: 1997
Architect: Atelier Hitoshi Abe
Project Team: Yoshikatsu Matsuno, Hideo Yaguchi, Hideyuki Mori
Structural Design: TIS & Partners
Contractors: Sugawara Construction + Nihon Jutaku Eizen

House +
Location: Susono-shi, Shizuoka Prefecture
Year: 1999
Architect: Atsushi Yagi Architects & Associates
Structural Consultant: Mikio Koshihara
General Contractor: Iizuka Construction Company

Weekend House
Location: Usui-gun, Gunma Prefecture
Year: 1998
Architect: Ryue Nishizawa / Office of Ryue Nishizawa
Structural Engineer: Structured Environment
Mechanical Engineer: System Design Laboratory
General Contractor: Niitsu Corporation

Villa Fuji
Location: Karuizawa-co, Nagano Prefecture
Year: 2000
Architect: Motomu Uno + Phase Architects
Structural Engineers: Masato Araya, Houshi Shibamura
Service Engineers: Masami Tan-no, Akhiro Nanjo
Landscape Architects: Tohru Mitani, Hiroharu Suzuki
Lighting Designer: Sachie Isaka
General Contractor: Kitano Construction Co., Ltd.

Illustration Credits

All illustrations were generously provided by the architects, unless otherwise specified. Photographic sources are listed where possible, but the publisher will endeavor to rectify any inadvertent omissions.

Numbers indicate page number.
t = top, b = bottom, l = left, c = center, r = right, ct = center top, cb = center bottom

Courtesy Atelier Hitoshi Abe: 196-200
Courtesy The Architectural Archives, University of Pennsylvania: 186b
Courtesy Tadao Ando Architects: 17
© Satoshi Arakawa: 143-149
© Shunichi Atsumi: 196-200
Courtesy Takamitsu Azuma: 15t
Courtesy Masaki Endoh + Masahiro Ikeda: 37bl
© Sadao Hibi: 9b, 15b, 59b, 60t
© Hiroyuki Hirai: 62-64, 66-69
© Katsuhisa Kida: 61, 76-81
© Toshiyuki Kobayashi: 174, 176-181
© Yoshiharu Matsumura: 150-157
© Mitsuo Matsuoka: 11b, 130-132, 134, 136-7
© Nacása & Partners inc: 50-54
© Nobuaki Nakagawa: 219t, 220-221
© Koji Okumura: 70, 72-75
Courtesy Naomi Pollock: 9t, 9c, 10t, 10c, 16, 59t, 60ct. 60cb,
60b, 141t, 141b
© Shinkenchiku-sha: 4, 10b, 18-20, 22-26, 28-36, 37br, 38, 41, 42-43,
45-49, 82, 84-89, 90-97, 103-108, 110-114, 116-120, 122-123, 124,
126-129, 158-166, 168-173, 188-190, 192-195, 202, 204-216, 218,
219b
Courtesy Yasuhiro Yamashita: 11t
© Makato Yoshida: 11c
Courtesy Junzo Yoshimura: 186t

Acknowledgements

I am extremely grateful to Karen Stein, Editorial Director at Phaidon Press, for taking on this book. I also wish to thank Julia Rydholm, the project editor at Phaidon Press, for her remarkable efforts and unflagging attention. In addition, I would like to thank the Photography Department at Shinkenchiku-sha Co. Ltd. for their cooperation and contribution.

The Graham Foundation and the Kajima Foundation provided me with much appreciated grant assistance. Throughout the process I was fortunate to have the ongoing encouragement of Richard Solomon, the Director of the Graham Foundation, and Robert Ivy, the Editor in Chief of Architectural Record magazine. I also wish to thank the architects whose works and words are included in this book as well as all the other designers whose insights and site visits were invaluable to me. Beverly Pollock and Beth Ungar gave me endless support and excellent suggestions. I know that George Pollock, who had a great love of the written word, would have appreciated this book.

It gives me great pleasure to dedicate this book to Abby, Eve and, most of all, David.

Phaidon Press Limited
Regent's Wharf
All Saints Street
London N1 9PA

Phaidon Press Inc.
180 Varick St.
New York, NY 10014

www.phaidon.com

First published 2005
© 2005 Phaidon Press Limited

ISBN 0 7148 4554 X

A CIP catalogue record for this book is available from the British Library.

Designed by 2x4
Printed in Hong Kong

Front and back cover: House in the Woods by Chiharu Sugi + Manami Takahashi / Plannet Works; Yamanashi Prefecture; Photographs: © Toshiyuki Kobayashi.